JOY
in the Brambles

ROSS H. PALFREYMAN

Publishing Services provided by Paper Raven Books LLC

Printed in the United States of America

First Printing, 2021

Library of Congress Control Number: 2023903154

Paperback ISBN: 979-8-9874094-4-2
Hardback ISBN: 979-8-9874094-0-4
Ebook ISBN: 979-8-9874094-1-1
Audio ISBN: 979-8-9874094-5-9

DEDICATION

To all who struggle through life's many brambles: Knowing the source of joy, or at least hoping that the source exists, can help you to experience joy even through the darkest of hours.

"Joy is the infallible sign of the presence of God."
-Pierre Teilhard de Chardin

Prologue

I remember a quiet evening some years ago that was interrupted by a telephone call from Bishop Chris Wilson. He asked me to speak to our congregation on the topic of missionary service. When I asked if there was anything specific he wanted me to touch on, he said no and that he would leave the specific subject matter to me. I had a few weeks to think it over, during which time I considered all the different things I did as a missionary. Service percolated to the top of my thoughts no matter what my initial thoughts were. I reflected on how many missionaries would say that their missionary service was the "best years of their lives." Friends and acquaintances said the same thing about serving in the Peace Corps, as did military veterans, who often noted that they learned a great deal and felt that they had a purpose when protecting the freedoms of fellow Americans.

Is there a common thread? I determined that, yes, there is. Service is that common thread. When people serve others there seems to be a sense of fulfillment, peace, and ultimately, joy. As this thought began to crystalize, I wondered if service needed to be a full-time occupation to bring peace and joy.

That led me to contemplate joy and happiness. Is one better than the other? Are they manifestations of the same thing? Attempts have been made to differentiate between the two by stating that joy is simply a deeper, more heartfelt emotion than happiness. However, as I played one against the other in my mind, it seemed that there was a significant difference between happiness and joy even though the difference was clouded by the extent of their seeming overlap.

As I formulated my thoughts for the talk that I was asked to give, I became more and more connected to the idea that service brings about fulfillment and joy. On the other hand, we can take actions to make our own lives happier. There are many actions we can take on our own behalf to make ourselves happy. For example, diet and exercise, which give us better control and use of our bodies and our time. Service, however, is directed toward the benefit of others. The uplifting feelings we get from service seem to be more internal in nature, an indwelling of feelings that I refer to as joy.

> *"I slept and dreamt that life was joy.*
> *I awoke and saw that life was service.*
> *I acted and behold, service was joy."*
> -Rabindranath Tagore

The conclusion that I came to is that there is an important distinction to be made between joy and happiness even though we tend to conflate the two. In reality, happiness comes from our efforts to please ourselves. Joy comes from our efforts to serve others. Both have value, but there is a distinction. And that distinction matters.

Our lives are filled with choices. Those choices are often influenced by what is going on around us: family squabbles, betrayal by friends real or perceived, political divides, and even self-inflicted wounds arising out of bad decisions or bad habits. Sometimes, not always, building or rebuilding happiness takes time to get in better physical or emotional shape. This requires inward reflection and attention. But at virtually any time, we can pursue and obtain joy simply by looking to and attending to the needs of others.

JOY

I am reminded of bramble bushes that can provide us with sweet fruits such as blackberries and raspberries. However, around those sweet fruits are prickly brambles that must be navigated. That does not mean we cannot get the fruit. It means only that we need to know how to move through the obstacles. Bears seem perfectly capable of bypassing the bramble bush's branches, shoots, and prickly barbs. They achieve their ultimate goal despite the thickets they encounter. Likewise, in our own lives, everything from personal tragedies to political upheavals create impediments to our obtaining joy. But joy is the ultimate fruit of our existence, and we are equipped to obtain it.

Understanding and navigating the pathways through the brambles of life to happiness and even joy, is the way we reach fulfillment in life. There are separate pathways to each. Understanding the pathways and the differences between the two makes it much easier to obtain both.

When we hear the word *just*, we traditionally think of *justice* and the law. Consequences for actions come to mind. But slowly, over time, this particular use of the word *just* has diminished and been replaced by the word *fair*. *Just* is now softer, less demanding of consequences for bad acts. It is now used more to announce our willingness to settle. *Just* has seemingly found a newer use, a limiting use, such as:

"Give me just a little more time;" meaning, we want a lot more time, but we will settle for a little more.

"Just one more slice of pizza;" meaning, we want the whole pizza, but we will settle for one more slice.

"If we can win just one more game;" meaning, we want to win them all, but we will settle for one more.

"We just want our children to be happy;" meaning, we know there is more, but we will settle for happy.

We can take more time, eat more pizza, and win more games, but what is it that surpasses happy—that we feel is out of reach, causing us to simply settle?

Books, essays, and debates abound arguing, explaining, and contending that joy is the prize beyond happiness. Many believe the common refrain that the way to reach joy is more exercise, better diet, more sleep, being more informed, and taking more time for oneself.

While that may be the common refrain, the refrain is wrong. It may bring additional happiness, but it does not elevate us or our children to the level of joy. The difference between happiness and joy is not a difference of degree. To achieve happiness, all attention is focused toward dealing with our approach to improving ourselves and our external experiences. One of the great writers of the Church of Jesus Christ of Latter-day Saints, Elder James E. Talmage describes pleasure as a tool of Satan while happiness:

"...springs from the deeper fountains of the soul and is not infrequently accompanied by tears."
-*Jesus the Christ,* Chapter 17, Note 2

Joy is viewed as a more heartfelt aspect of happiness without regard for a deeper differentiation of one from the other. But that is exactly what needs to be insisted upon. While the depth of the feeling is something to be acknowledged, it masks the more important difference. The downside to blurring the distinction between the two is that the senses become dulled to the possibility that joy can elevate life to a more fulfilling, even a more noble sphere. My sense is that what Talmage was really trying to describe was the difference between happiness and joy.

It has been written that:

> *"…man is that he might have joy."*
> *-Book of Mormon, 2 Nephi 2:25*

Joy springs out of selflessness. Joy requires outward focus on the needs of others. Joy is spiritually sourced.

Happiness, by stark contrast, has its roots in inward thinking. Happiness involves fulfilling our own needs and desires. More exercise, better diet, and a more informed life may make us happy, but it isn't really focused on anyone else. This does not mean that happiness is bad. It is differently focused.

An example of the confusion between the two is easy to see here. If we serve in a soup kitchen, we might walk away saying it made us happy. But the trigger for the feeling came from an orientation toward the needs of others. Therefore, the feeling would be better described as joy. Recognizing the different sources of happiness and joy helps us to return to the experience of joy by engaging in more opportunities for service.

In this world of hatred, greed, and selfishness, *just* how do we obtain joy? Is there a God who would create a world where joy is the goal, and yet there is no way to achieve it? Death, horrific accidents, crime, disease, pandemics, and wars all appear to belie the notion that there is a loving God, desirous of joy for all of us. How could God create a world where all of these bad things seem to stand in the way of our destiny, to wit, joy?

In the end, we get to choose, on a very personal and individual level, whether to settle for *just* happiness, where we are constantly fretting over our own well-being, or to strive for joy, wherein we set-aside our constant desire for self-fulfillment in favor of trying to address the needs of others. It is quite simple really. Both can be pursued, but sometimes not at the same time.

It isn't that happiness and joy are mutually exclusive or that one is necessarily better than the other. Rather, it is that they are quite different in their focus, and it is imperative to understand the difference in order to enjoy all that life has to offer. If the path is not clearly matched to the process, then achieving the goal of either happiness or joy becomes practically impossible. Like a ship at sea without a captain, map, compass, or a clearly defined destination, the ultimate goal is left to chance, and the ship is likely to end up in the wrong port or possibly in no port at all.

There is an apocryphal story that when John Lennon, the famous Beatle, was five years old, his mother would tell him that happiness was the key to life. When he went to school, he reportedly was asked what he wanted to be when he grew up. He wrote down the word *happy*. His teacher then told him that he did not understand the assignment. John Lennon's response was to tell the teacher that she did not understand life. We are often easily distracted from our real goals and purposes by false assumptions about what we are really after.

While we have some control over happiness by internally satisfying our desires, we have even more control over joy. Joy comes from God. It comes from our service to others, our empathy toward others, and our willingness to be charitable. It is as if we see God in others. As Pollyanna was told in the Walt Disney movie of the same name:

"We looked for the good in them, and we found it."
-Pollyanna

During a dinner party some years ago, the challenges of child rearing were being discussed. Our guests were the parents of two boys. We talked about problems with curfew, bad friends, inappropriate language, etc. Slowly the conversation turned to one of our friends' sons who was a special kind of challenge. He was very intelligent and very restless. I had coached him for a couple of years and knew him well. He was one of my favorites but truly a challenge to control.

Then, out of the blue, the mother of this boy observed that our children were better equipped to fit into society and live life more fully because of their religious training. "You have your church," I believe is the way she put it. There was a real advantage to a religious background in her mind's eye. Her husband then agreed. It provided a program for moral education and a process for reaching out. They were right; a faith-based community can provide opportunities for service that we might not otherwise be aware of. However, the price was high in that it required church attendance and adherence to certain moral principles.

I was flabbergasted by the comment. These friends are highly intelligent, well-educated, and very successful financially and socially. I respect them greatly and always had great fun with them. It is not as if they were not allowed to participate in a faith-based community or weren't aware of its advantages; they just chose not to be involved in religion, in spite of seeing the value it could bring into their lives and into the lives of their children. What was the value of religion that they saw but decided not to partake of? It was as if the choice was between religion or Napa Valley wine tasting trips, congregational worship or Sunday morning surfing excursions, or other inwardly focused pleasures.

On the surface, their lives were great and something I occasionally envied. Perhaps there were too many choices. The world offers all kinds of opportunities to be happy. The opportunities were readily available to these well-to-do folks. They bought "*just* happy" as sufficient for them. Looking back, they seemed to recognize that there was more.

Sometimes our circumstances act to prevent us from recognizing and then choosing the pathway to joy. Jesus Christ spoke in the New Testament of an interest that is beyond one's self and that points outward toward the needs of others:

> "*And, behold, one came and said unto him, Good Master, what good thing shall I do, that I may have eternal life? And he said unto him, Why callest thou me good? There is none good but one, that is God: but if thou wilt enter into life, keep the commandments.*
>
> *He saith unto him, Which? Jesus said, Thou shalt do no murder, Thou shalt not commit adultery, Thou shalt not steal, Thou shalt not bear false witness, Honour thy father and thy mother: and, Thou shalt love thy neighbour as thyself. The young man saith unto him, all these things have I kept from my youth up: what lack I yet?*
>
> *Jesus said unto him, if thou wilt be perfect, go and sell that thou hast, and give to the poor, and thou shalt have treasure in heaven: and come and follow me.*
>
> *But when the young man heard that saying, he went away sorrowful: for he had great possessions.*
>
> *Then said Jesus unto his disciples, Verily I say unto you, That a rich man shall hardly enter into the kingdom of heaven.*

*And again I say unto you, It is easier for a camel to go
through the eye of a needle, than for a rich man to enter
into the kingdom of God."*
-Matthew 19:16-24

(Note: All biblical references herein come from the King James translation)

Jesus did not seem to have had anything at all against the rich man. He did not criticize his riches or how the rich man obtained them, and he didn't ask if he had paid enough taxes. In fact, he seemed to accept the rich man's assertion that he followed the commandments. But all of those things related to inward thinking, focusing on the rich man's own physical and emotional needs. The rich man controlled his own life and obeyed the commandments. His life was in order. The fact that Jesus invited the rich man to follow him, indicated a certain amount of respect for the rich man. After all, how many people did Jesus invite individually to follow him? Very few is the answer. Just think, if the rich man had accepted the invitation, we probably would know him by name instead of having to refer to him as the "rich man." But by asking the rich man to sell his possessions and "give to the poor," Jesus was asking for something else, something more. Jesus wanted the rich man to focus outwardly instead of inwardly. Jesus was offering joy.

Because of his wealth, the rich man had many opportunities to be happy. He was so secure in the worldly aspects of life that he could not adjust the focus of his attention from his worldly possessions to the needs of those around him. He trusted in himself for happiness. He settled. He could not let go of the inward focus toward his own comfort and happiness to embrace what Jesus had in store for him, which was service to others and the joy that arises from it.

Introspection can lead to self-improvement. It can increase our capacity for more. Once we secure some degree of happiness, we need to then transition to the pursuit of joy which requires outward service. Our attention in the secular world seems almost always to be pointed inward, just like the rich man's. That is the wrong direction by 180°.

The lesson of the rich man in the New Testament is that the more riches you have, the more independent from God you may feel. The more choices you have, the more selfishly you tend to think. (After all, your worldly possessions take time to monitor and shepherd and that is time that you might otherwise use to focus on the needs of others). Wealth accumulation and spiritual development both require focus. Focus is time sensitive and therefore limited. Jesus was teaching that the ultimate goal is joy and that takes outward focus.

What's interesting about looking outward is that it not only impacts the receiver of the service directly, but it also tends to impact others going forward. It has a rippling effect. Joy is quite often contagious. How many times has someone held a door open for us, we smile and then hold the door open for the next person? Such a small act, and yet that simple act is passed on. No act of charity is too small.

Interestingly, we hear stories from our friends and others about some event that was very funny to them. It made them happy. It made them laugh. At the end of the story, when no one else laughs, the storyteller then concludes with, "I guess you had to be there." Happiness is a pretty singular, inward event. By contrast, when someone tells a story that filled their heart with joy, sharing that story can actually convey the joy. The receiver of the story can feel it. He did not have to be there to feel the connection that resulted from an outward reach by one person to another.

THE PENCIL BOX

Years ago, my son Sam was in the second grade. We were nearing the end of the year at Arroyo Vista Elementary School in South Pasadena, and it was time for the big open house. I generally let my wife handle open houses as I have never been a big fan of meetings, and I especially disdain them when they're optional. But on this occasion, Claralyn prevailed upon me and I went. When I do attend open houses, I usually wander from classroom to classroom, not really paying too much attention to the teachers' explanations of what happened during the year. It drives my wife crazy as she is a fourth grade teacher. She considers it rude behavior. I say all of this to point out that my attention was lacking, and I had low expectations for the evening.

When my son's second grade teacher, Mr. Dahlberg, finished his presentation, I wandered into the room and around the desks looking for Sam's. Not knowing what to do once I found Sam's desk, I sat down in his little chair and began going through his things. Out from the bowels of the desk I pulled a rather gaudy Star Wars pencil box. I had never seen the pencil box before and after fidgeting with it for a few minutes, I noticed that Mr. Dahlberg had approached and was looking down at me. He smiled and asked if I knew the story behind the pencil box. I did not. He continued, "I think you will like the story."

One of Sam's classmates had entered the second grade without being able to read. Early in the year, Mr. Dahlberg was fearful that he would have to hold this boy back for another year of second grade so that he could catch up to grade level in his reading. But then something happened. Sam, without any prodding or even a mention, began to tutor his classmate in reading. They often stayed in at recess and at lunch time to read together. As Mr. Dahlberg continued telling me about Sam sacrificing his time to help his classmate, Mr. Dahlberg's eyes began to water.

He said that he had never seen a student sacrifice so much time and energy to help a classmate. Mr. Dahlberg lamented that there was no way that he would have been able to spend enough time with this particular student without sacrificing time needed for the rest of the class. By the time of the open house, this classmate of Sam's had caught up to grade level with his reading skills, and Mr. Dahlberg was thrilled that he was going to be able to pass him on to the third grade.

By now, tears were freely flowing down Mr. Dahlberg's cheeks as he went on to explain that he had reported Sam's work to the student's parents throughout the year. The parents were so grateful that they had gone out and purchased this Star Wars pencil box to give to Sam in recognition of and gratitude for his good works with their son. By the end of the story, Mr. Dahlberg was filled with joy that had come to him by observing the service given by Sam. I too was stricken with the sense that something wonderful had happened. Sam was not even present in the room at the time, and yet his service, his charity, had clearly overwhelmed Mr. Dahlberg and had me completely choked up as I spun the pencil box around in my hands with a new appreciation for my son and what the pencil box meant.

Service to others, without any expectation of return, brings joy not only to those served and to those who receive the service, but it reverberates out like ripples on the water, to provide joy to those who come in contact with that service. Whether at the time of the service or at any time later, the result of service is joy.

BALANCE

I like my chocolate. If I control it, it won't kill me. If I don't…then there is something else in store. Alcohol and many other self-indulgent habits can also fall into this category. The danger in the pursuit of happiness to an extreme is that it can become an end in itself and take you away from the pursuit of joy.

We become accustomed to a certain level of one pleasurable experience or another, and we need either increased amounts of a wider variety of those pleasurable experiences to find the happiness or satisfaction we seek. Good things can become bad things very quickly when they become the sole focus of our lives. There are many good things to be had and shared by way of happiness, but happiness as the sole or primary focus tends quickly to devolve into selfish, self-destructive behaviors that ultimately compromise both happiness and joy. In our consumer-oriented world, marketing encourages consumption through Pavlovian conditioning, promising happiness through psychochemical responses to supernormal stimuli. Desire is as old as time, but we have learned how to manipulate it for gain with unprecedented efficiency. That cultivated desire to consume can distract us from joy.

In measured amounts, things that bring us pleasure and happiness can and do add to the richness of life. Exercise gives the body vitality. Reading can bring us to a better understanding of the world and/or allow for a temporary escape from the stresses of the day, depending on what you are reading. Even dieting can make us feel better so long as an occasional Double Stuf Oreo can be included.

In religion generally, joy is the actual end game, not happiness. But it has sometimes blurred the critical distinction between the words happiness and joy. Instead of focusing on the <u>distinctly different sources</u> for happiness and joy, the terms are distinguished only by degree, missing the whole point of the difference. Once the <u>distinct sources</u> for happiness and joy are identified, it becomes easy to understand that joy is dramatically more spiritual in the long run. When we look at this more closely, we see that the difference is really quite important to the fulfillment of our human potential and satisfaction in life.

> *"When you do things from your soul, you feel a river*
> *moving in you, a joy."*
> -Jalal ad-Din Mohammad Rumi

There are at least three characteristics that lead us to joy: caring, compassion, and charity. These three characteristics overlap, combine, and tie us to each other through service. Together, they bring joy to our lives.

CARING

Caring is the first characteristic and is foundational. We must be able to actually recognize the needs of those around us. This implies more than just awareness, though. It requires a full sense of empathy—the ability to put ourselves in the position of others. Instead of simply worrying about the status of our own lives, we show our caring for others by feeling and by exhibiting concern and empathy for others.

> *"They may not need me: but they might. I'll let my head*
> *be just in sight: a smile as small as mine might be precisely,*
> *their necessity."*
> -Emily Dickinson

Caring involves the sacrifice of personal, self-indulgent thought in favor of empathetic projection toward others. In the Christian world Jesus Christ was the greatest example of sacrifice. He gave his entire life to redeem all of mankind:

> *"Greater love hath no man than this, that a man lay*
> *down his life for his friends."*
> -John 15:13

SOME CLOTHES

It was several years ago when I was serving in a bishopric in a congregation for The Church of Jesus Christ of Latter-day Saints in South Pasadena, California. Dominique, a young boy from a poor part of East Los Angeles, was a part of our congregation. He turned 12 and was ready to receive the Aaronic Priesthood, which meant that he was going to be allowed to pass the sacrament to the congregation, among other things. The ordination took place but for several weeks I did not see him passing the sacrament. I pulled Dominique aside and asked him if there was a problem. He sheepishly reported that he felt uncomfortable passing the sacrament in the kind of clothes that he had available to him, to wit, Levis and a plaid shirt. I had not thought about his wardrobe at all. I had been happy for his ordination, but I hadn't displayed any caring.

I mentioned my conversation with Dominique to my wife, Claralyn. She immediately conveyed the obvious solution which was to simply take Dominque out and buy him a white shirt and tie. Why hadn't I thought of that? Was I too busy with my own life to see Dominique's needs and then care enough to do something about it? Empathy was not in me. The easy and painfully correct answer was that I did not seem to care enough to notice Dominque's needs and then find a solution.

Thanks to Claralyn, I picked up our new deacon at his home and we embarked on a shopping journey to Nordstrom in Glendale. At first,

I was looking to buy him a white shirt and tie. But as our shopping venture progressed, I was having too much fun watching Dominique marvel at his new acquisitions to stop there. He was ecstatic. I was filled with a sense that I was doing something truly worthwhile. We got the shirt and tie, and then added a pair of slacks and shoes and, well, everything.

> *"There is no joy in possession without sharing."*
> -Erasmus of Rotterdam

That next Sunday, I watched a confident, young man pass the sacrament for the first time. I was euphoric. When I was asked by the bishop if I wanted to be reimbursed for the clothes, my response was surprisingly swift! The answer was "NO!" I had no desire to give up the good feelings—the joy that I had from this act of service—for a couple of bucks. I was not looking for financial reimbursement. That would have robbed me of my experience of caring and being able to provide something for someone else, without any expectation of a return. Besides, I didn't make these kinds of good choices often, so I felt like I needed to hold on to this one.

TAUGHT BY A CHILD

Somehow, the lesson taught by my experience with Dominique did not sink in as well as you would think. Some years later, I was coaching a Little League baseball team at Riddle Field in Laguna Beach, California. During a game, I had a lapse in judgement. I allowed my competitive nature to overcome my sense of caring. I had inherited a pretty good baseball team from the year before and would be competitive with almost anyone that I drafted to fill out the roster.

Therefore, I decided to be a builder for the next couple of years, and I drafted three 10-year-olds with my first three draft picks to play in the 10- to 12-year-old league. These three 10-year-olds were the best available 10-year-olds in the league (with the exception of a couple of boys whose fathers were coaching other teams. If I could have drafted them out from under their fathers, I would have). The season went by and we won our local Laguna Beach Little League championship. We were then invited to play in the Tournament of Champions for Orange County.

Vivid in my mind is the semi-final game: we were down four to two with our last at bat. The opposition's pitcher was a very good 12-year-old, and we were having a difficult time hitting off of him. We had a runner on first base and one out, and it was easy to see that my 12-year-old player at bat was going down by way of the dreaded strikeout. That would mean there would be two men out when my on-deck batter went up to the plate to hit. My on-deck hitter was also a 12-year-old but may well have been my weakest player. I looked down the bench and called young 10-year-old Roy Herbert to come over so we could talk. He was a really good hitter, even as a 10-year-old. We spoke briefly and I told him to get a helmet because he was going to pinch hit for the on-deck 12-year-old batter. He walked away excited that he was going to get an opportunity to bat in this big situation. A moment later he returned with his helmet and bat in hand and then he taught me a lesson I have never forgotten:

He said, "Coach, [12-year-old's name omitted] is probably never going to play baseball again after this season. This may be his last opportunity to bat in his life. I am going to be here another couple of years. Shouldn't we let him hit?"

His query stopped me cold in my tracks. It was as if the game was suspended all of a sudden. The entire event took on a whole new meaning to me. Of course, Roy was right, but I really wanted to win. As my mind quickly went through my choices and options, I realized I really did not have any choices or options that made any sense other than to follow Roy's admonition that came to me in the form of a question. Roy had hit the nail on the head, driving a stake through my heart. What was important was that each of the boys had opportunities for good experiences. Winning wasn't everything, even though up to that moment it had been the only thing to me. Roy cared about his teammate.

Roy and I stood side by side as the 12-year-old batter stepped up to the plate after the second out had been recorded by way of strikeout. The game was on the line, there were two outs, and it was highly unlikely that this 12-year-old batter was even going to be able to foul off a pitch from this excellent pitcher. I would love to say that our 12-year-old batter came through and hit a two-run homerun to tie the game, which would be the case if this were a Hallmark movie. Unfortunately, the fact of the matter is that he struck out just as I had anticipated he would. The strange thing is that I didn't feel nearly as badly as I thought I would. Roy had taught me a most valuable lesson—that I should be looking to the needs of others and then serving those needs, rather than pursuing my own selfish ambitions. I had a choice. Roy Herbert helped me care and make the right choice.

This Roy Herbert event marks a clear choice between inwardly thinking about what would make me happy or outwardly caring enough about someone else to recognize and address their needs. I could have been happy if I let Roy bat and he got a hit. Selfishly, I wanted to win. Instead, Roy helped me care about his teammate. There is a distinction here and it matters.

> *"All I have are the choices I make."*
> *-The Adjustment Bureau*

An existentialist would say "existence precedes essence." We must choose without greater knowledge of the impact of our actions. Would the team's delight in winning the game have superseded that boy's disappointment at not batting one last time? Is the other team's victory a good thing? Is the potential for joy or despair equal among all participants in the game? What about parents and friends? How will this decision impact the sense of identity and self-confidence for each of these players? There are no easy answers, but caring and empathy can provide insights that logic alone cannot. Sometimes happiness and joy can be accomplished together. Sometimes we have to make a choice. Roy taught me that we cannot always have it both ways.

Another story illustrates that these opportunities to care are all around us virtually all of the time if we just take the time to look. We need to adjust our mindset to be turned toward caring for others instead of constantly worrying about our own needs and desires. The following was provided by a friend on my Facebook page:

"Yesterday, Matt was sick. I picked up Archie from the sitter and Eloise from school and decided to run to Target for a few things. I had hoped to be in and out quickly.

I found a line with just one person ahead of me and began organizing my items on the conveyer. After placing my items, I looked up to see that the person ahead of me was an elderly woman. She was paying for her items with change and wanted to purchase each separately. The part of me that had a long day at work, the part of me who had a one and a half year old having a meltdown in the car, the part of me that had set an unnecessary timeline for Target and getting home, was frustrated with this woman and the inconvenience she had placed on me.

But then I watched the young employee with this woman. I watched him help her count her change, ever so tenderly taking it from her shaking hands. I listened to him repeatedly saying "yes, ma'am" to her. When she asked if she had enough to buy a reusable bag, he told her she did and went two lines over to get one for her and then repacked her items. Never once did this employee huff, gruff, or roll his eyes. He was nothing but patient and kind.

As I was watching him, I saw that Eloise was too. She was standing next to the woman, watching the employee count the change. I realized that I hadn't been inconvenienced at all. My daughter was instead witnessing kindness and patience and being taught this valuable lesson by a complete stranger. Furthermore, I realized that I, too, needed a refresher on this lesson. When the woman was finished, the employee began ringing up my items and thanked me for my patience. I then thanked him for teaching us patience and kindness by his treatment of that elderly woman. And although my timeline for Target was askew, when he was finished, I pushed my cart through the store trying to find the manager. I wanted her to know of the employee's kindness and patience and how much it meant to me. After tracking her down and sharing the story with her, we left Target with a cart full of consumable items, but what is more, a heart full of gratitude for such an invaluable lesson.

If we see God in others' goodness, such behavior becomes easier for us."

THE CAR

My brother Eric was living in South Pasadena, California where he was a student working nights to try to support his young family. His financial condition was similar to most students' financial situations: dire. Unfortunately, his ramshackle car finally broke down and died at a most inopportune time.

The bishop of his church congregation heard about Eric's challenge. The bishop happened to have an older car that was still serviceable. One night Eric heard a knock at his door and upon answering it, invited the bishop into his apartment. A visit from the bishop often means that you are in the process of being asked to perform some kind of service in the congregation such as teaching a Sunday school class or helping with the operation of one of the various organizations within the congregation.

However, on this evening, the bishop related to Eric that he had heard of the loss of Eric's family vehicle. Eric confirmed that this was the case. The bishop then stood in the middle of the living room, walked over to Eric and asked Eric for $1.00 to make the transaction legal. Somewhat bewildered about what was happening, Eric dutifully handed the bishop $1.00, and the bishop relinquished his car keys to my brother.

Still somewhat baffled, but slowly coming to a realization of what was happening, Eric asked the bishop for confirmation of what was actually transpiring. The bishop confirmed that he was indeed providing Eric with a mode of transportation so that he could continue working and attending school and that he did not really want anything in return. After thanking the bishop for this gracious gift and then asking if there was anything the bishop needed, Eric saw the bishop to the door and then finally asked, "Well, don't you need a ride home?"

In so many words, the bishop's response was that he would rather walk home so that he could spend a little time and bask in the light that had been generated by his doing the right thing, the kind thing, the caring thing. Seeing to the needs of someone else, realizing that he could do something about it, and then actually acting upon that knowledge to lighten someone else's burden were all things to reflect on. With that, the bishop walked down the street and into the dark night. Acts of service almost always result in joy whether that joy is something that other people see and revel in or if it is simply etched in our own hearts; joy is the result and it lasts.

"What we do in life echoes in eternity."
-Gladiator

COMPASSION

The American Heritage Dictionary defines compassion as "Deep awareness of the suffering of another coupled with the wish to relieve it." As we become aware of people and their needs, we become more compassionate toward them because we are more understanding of their needs. With understanding, we become less inclined to judge others' circumstances and why they may have needs in the first place.

Joy in our lifetime is possible and in fact is God's goal for us, but we have to be able to see past our own selfish pursuit of happiness so that we can actually be aware of the needs of others and then act for the good of our neighbors. Again, our attention must point to others, not inwardly toward ourselves. Shouldn't the promise of God's joy motivate us? We need to reflect on whether or not our acts are for the betterment of our neighbors or if they are intended to attend to our own needs first. Only God can see into our hearts to make the judgement of our intent. That is why we are to leave judgment to God:

> *"Judge not, that ye be not judged. For with what judg-ment ye judge, ye shall be judged: and with what measure ye mete, it shall be measured to you again.*
>
> *And why beholdest thou the mote that is in thy brother's eye, but considereth not the beam that is in thine own eye?"*
> *-Matthew 7:1-3*

The warning against judging others isn't just to protect those we might be inclined to judge. Judging others poses at least four problems. The first is that we do not know what motivates others, which often leads us to misjudge. The second is that we spend time and attention judging, which then causes us to miss opportunities to serve. The third problem is that we channel too much energy into remembering why we made the judgement. The fourth reason is that our own judgement becomes fixated in our minds and makes it almost impossible to see the other person in a compassionate light. Our time is limited and all of it should be positively used:

> *"People are often unreasonable and self-centered, forgive them anyway. If you are kind, people may accuse you of ulterior motives. Be kind anyway. If you are honest, people may cheat you. Be honest anyway. If you find happiness, people may be jealous. Be happy anyway. The good you do today may be forgotten tomorrow. Do good anyway. Give the world the best you have and it may never be enough. Give your best anyway. For you see, in the end, it is between you and God. It was never between you and them anyway."*
> -Mother Theresa

Judging our own motives is enough of a challenge. We do not have time nor do we have the ability to judge others. I like to use the following example to show our limited ability to judge:

Imagine a 14-year-old boy helping an elderly lady across a busy street. Why might he be performing the act? Consider these possible explanations:

1. He's a Boy Scout looking to get a merit badge for himself or he's a Boy Scout who is already an Eagle Scout and has learned to enjoy helping the elderly;

2. He's trying to impress the girl sitting at the café across the way or he's trying to get the elderly lady to her granddaughter;

3. He's trying to steal her wallet or he's helping the elderly lady at her request.

The point is that what motivates the 14-year-old boy is between God and the boy—and nobody else. Our own lives provide enough opportunities for judgement without looking to judge the motives of others.

> *"Our job is to love others without stopping to inquire whether or not they are worthy."*
> -Thomas Merton

What really motivates our actions? Do we utilize caring, compassion, and charity to serve others or do we act for ourselves, for our own happiness? We should worry about the direction of our own actions and not anybody else's.

> *"The purpose of religion is to control yourself, not to criticize others."*
> -Dalai Lama

Compassion involves even more than a simple absence of judgement and implies that your actions are driven by a sense of love, rather than simply the execution of a commandment or a duty.

Regardless of gender, race, national origin, or religion, each of us can lay claim to being one of God's children. Gentleness, shown through politeness and kindness expressed in an elegant way, shows respect and love to those we come in contact with. Some call these manners.

"Therefore all things whatsoever ye would that men should do to you, do ye even so to them: for this is the law and the prophets."
-Matthew 7:12

This presumes that all others wish to be treated as you do. Empathy extends the golden rule to understanding others, giving rise to actions on their behalf.

The drummer for the famous Beatles, Ringo Star, tells a story of how compassion was exemplified by his friend George Harrison:

"I went to see George [Harrison] in Switzerland in his last weeks. He was very ill from lung and brain cancer. My daughter, Lee, was also ill with a brain tumor. I said, 'George, I love you, but Lee is going into the hospital in Boston and I've got to go there.' He said, 'Do you want me to come with you?' He couldn't move, but, in his being, he was willing. He was just that good of a friend."
-AARP *Magazine*, October/November 2015, Pg. 16

After caring comes compassion, which seems to be an action word or at least indicates a willingness to act.

EARTHQUAKE

The 1994 Northridge earthquake literally rocked my family's world. Our chimney fell onto the neighbor's driveway, just barely missing their Jaguar. Pictures came off the walls, the house swayed wildly, and the chandelier danced rhythmically in the dining room almost touching the ceiling as it swayed back and forth. Nevertheless, we were unharmed, and we ate breakfast after a short bit of excited reflecting.

I then remembered good friends who happened to live in Northridge, at the epicenter of the earthquake. I tried to call them on the telephone, but their home line was down. Their cell phone was also out of service. My wife and I talked it over and decided that I should get in the car and take a drive, just in case.

It's about a 25 to 30 minute drive from Pasadena to Northridge—the much maligned Los Angeles freeways are actually pretty efficient when it comes to tying Los Angeles communities together. But on this day, one of the freeway overpasses that I would normally use had collapsed. That meant surface streets were the only alternatives—a not-so-swift means of traversing from community to community in Los Angeles. I worked my way toward the San Fernando Valley. After travelling through parts of town I had never seen before, I finally began to sense that I was getting close. I turned up a street toward the Sorensen's home in Northridge. As soon as I made the right-hand turn, I was confronted by flames shooting out of the middle of the street...a gas main had broken. I was blocked. So I travelled down a few more streets and tried turning right again. This time, I was blocked by a veritable river flowing down the street from a major break in a water main. I moved on down a few more streets, and ultimately, I found a street that was clear and headed up the hill in search of the Sorensens.

As I drove up their street, it was eerily quiet. Sitting on the curb outside of her home, I found Stephanie holding her head in her hands. Her children had been sent down the hill to a safer location. John was inside surveying the damage. I pulled over, got out of the car, and then sat down next to Stephanie on the curb. Stephanie was clearly shaken and had no desire to go back into the house. We talked. After some time went by, she was ready and we got up and went into the house to assess the damage and see what could be salvaged. Inside, we joined John. There was some gallows humor type comments made in an effort to cut the horrific fog of feelings at the scene of the living disaster. With each aftershock, and there were many, the query was whether or not "the big one" would be next. We prioritized what should be done first, then next, and so on.

My first recollection was viewing the wall that separated the kitchen from the dining room. What once was a straight wall had literally been re-engineered by the earthquake to the shape of an S. Had it been designed as an S-shaped wall in the first place, it would have been very cool. But knowing that the wall was not architecturally engineered that way, it was unnerving to look at something that had become so contorted. On the other side of the room from that S-shaped wall was their refrigerator. The shaking had been so extreme that the refrigerator had actually tipped over. Apparently, while it was tipping over, the refrigerator door opened and as it fell, the door hit the floor first stopping the refrigerator from hitting the ground. It ended up at almost a 45-degree angle which meant that everything inside the refrigerator slid out onto the floor with broken glass and food everywhere. Most of the cupboards had likewise been emptied out onto the countertops and onto the floor. The house had been completely trashed.

The Sorensen's chimney had fallen onto the neighbor's home and into the neighbor's bedroom where the neighbors had been asleep. They narrowly missed being crushed.

John could only stay briefly as he was an administrator at a skilled nursing facility and had to leave to tend to staff and many of the elderly whose life-sustaining hospital equipment had stopped operating due to the power outage.

Stephanie and I started to feel a little bit more comfortable about going through the rubble and retrieving what we could from their home when a significant aftershock struck. That was the end of our work for the day. Stephanie was out of the house and into the street before the aftershock was over.

The chaos of the moment was overwhelming. We sat on the curb outside of the Sorensen's home and tried to relax. We started the day as very good friends. Our shared experience of the day cemented our relationship as lifetime friends. Because there was an underlying caring and compassion for the needs of others, joy came out of an otherwise tragic experience. The entire load of the horrific Northridge earthquake was not carried by one person alone. I had acted on my caring with some compassion. The experience was helpful to and appreciated by the Sorensens, but was actually more fulfilling to me: I felt joy in tending to the pains of someone else. Any of my concerns about my own home and its status simply vanished as I tended to the needs of the Sorensens. The lesson here is that seeing to the needs of others through service lightens the burdens of our own lives.

THE SMALL LESSONS

A minor tragedy in my own professional life has occurred on two separate occasions with two very different responses by me, resulting in two very different outcomes. As an attorney, I do a significant amount of dictating that I then turn over to an assistant who transcribes the dictation into the written word for me. It comprises a significant part of my work product.

Some five years or so into my legal practice, an assistant accidently erased my dictation before it could be transcribed. I would be lying if I told you that I enjoyed the news. While I did not react by screaming or yelling at my assistant, my reaction was actually more immature. For days, I sulked, pouted, and generally made sure that my assistant felt badly about the event. She did. I made her life miserable for no good reason. It certainly accomplished nothing. It only magnified the angst of the error. Unfortunately, compassion was far from my mind.

Some years later, my two sons, Sam and John, went on a Boy Scout hike. One of their Scout leaders relayed a story to me of an experience that he observed during the hike. Sam and John were assigned to cook a morning meal together. They had to start a fire (without matches) to boil water as a part of the cooking assignment. They were at high altitude which meant that the boiling point for water was achieved at a lower temperature than normal. Hence, everything had to be cooked longer.

Sam got the fire started and got the water boiling. John had then begun to pour the breakfast ingredients into the pot of boiling water when, by accident, he tipped the pot of water over onto the fire, extinguishing it. Sam's reaction could have been to harshly criticize John for spilling the water onto the fire. He could have thrown up his hands in disgust and told John to redo the task by himself. (I would have done all those things and probably more. Just ask my brothers.) As the story has been told to me, Sam did none of those things. Instead, he calmly instructed John to go down to the river and collect more water while he restarted the fire. The process of cooking that meal went on without further incident. There were no harsh words, feelings, or lingering resentment one way or the other. They just went on. Sam's caring and compassion in the situation minimized any negative consequences. Compassion can easily defuse potentially dramatic events. But it means looking to the feelings and needs of others above the impact of life's events on you. I have often thought of that story and have had occasion to apply the lesson of that story to my own life. Sometimes I am more successful than others.

I experienced another instance where a different assistant of mine erased some of my dictation before it was transcribed. This time, my mind immediately reflected upon the Sam and John incident, and I determined that Sam's was the response that I should mirror rather than the pettiness I'd shown with the previous assistant.

I remembered the goodness of Sam's reaction to John's losing the hot water and dousing of the fire. He cared about John and had compassion for the situation. Instead of making an unnecessary judgement, he simply moved on. And so, I changed my behavior. As a result of the second erasing incident, I realized that the assistant already felt awful enough without any help from me. She apologized and that was the end of it. We moved on. There was no recrimination, no pouting, or lasting sense of bitterness. This time, I cared about what had happened to my assistant. I had compassion for the embarrassment that she felt, and therefore did not make matters worse. In fact, responding in that way, the negative impact of the situation was minimized for both of us. I was concerned more about her reaction to the mistake than what I would need to do to re-dictate the erased work. We both won. Compassion is good.

> *"Some believe it is only great power that can hold evil in check. But that is not what I have found. I have found that it is the small everyday deeds of ordinary folk that keep the darkness at bay. Small acts of kindness and love."*
> -J.R.R. Tolkien, *The Lord of the Rings*

Gandalf recognized that small acts of kindness can have a huge impact on evil. It is not always the grand gesture that accomplishes good. Jesus Christ showed that in his washing of the apostles' feet at the Last Supper. The act itself was small. The symbolism of his caring and compassion for the apostles was a grand gesture. It was not necessary that Christ perform some great miracle. He was able to convey his love for the apostles through this small act of kindness.

As has often been said, "lift where you stand." Do the good you can where you are, when you can do it, and how you can do it.

THE TEDDY BEAR

Abe Oyler, a good friend, related one of his own experiences that confirms that the impact of small acts of caring and compassion can last through the ages:

"In 1987 I was in kindergarten at Carmel River School. My oldest brother, Ben, had died a year prior from AIDS. (He was nine). It was a scary time in the world to face AIDS. Very little was known about it. Some kids were told to stay away from me. I was teased, called words I didn't understand. Kids would scream out that I had AIDS and run away. Hard to cope with at age five. I responded in kind, acting out, teasing, and being mean. I found that I got more attention through my negative actions. I felt so very alone. One day, my kindergarten teacher held me back from recess saying that someone wanted to give me a present. There was a lady I had never met before. She gave me a teddy bear that she had made by hand. I remember thinking it was a bit creepy looking, but there it sat in my room for thirteen more years. This kind woman had heard about my brother and wanted to do something nice for me.

Today, I was unpacking some boxes in the garage and

*found my teddy bear. A wave of memories and feelings
of gratitude come rushing over me. I have kept this teddy
bear for twenty-eight years. It is a symbol of love and kindness. A simple and beautiful gift that still reminds me of
my brother. To the woman who made this for me, I don't
remember your name, but I love you!"*

These acts can bring about heaven on earth, can bring light into the darkness and lift the lives of those around us.

*"Darkness cannot drive out darkness; only light can do
that. Hate cannot drive out hate; only love can do that."*
-Martin Luther King, Jr.

CHARITY

Ultimately, there is charity, the third step towards joy. It directs all your positive energy toward those around you. Charity, of course, includes a far broader sweep of concepts than simply the idea of positive energy. While all of these steps—caring, compassion and charity—are important, charity is what represents the highest level of love and service. Charity is central to joy. This is best described in the apostle Paul's first epistle to the Corinthians:

> *"Though I speak with the tongues of men and of angels,*
> *and have not charity, I am become as sounding brass, or*
> *a tinkling cymbal. And though I have the gift of prophesy,*
> *and understand all mysteries, and all knowledge; and*
> *though I have all faith, so that I can remove mountains,*
> *and have not charity, I am nothing. And though I bestow*
> *all my goods to feed the poor and though I give my body to*
> *be burned, and have not charity it profit of me nothing."*
> *I Corinthians 13:1-3*

In this passage, Paul makes clear that the other Christian virtues, while noteworthy, are not sufficient. They will not bring us fullness nor will they bring us fully into the presence of God's light. They will not provide a whole and direct encounter with God's joy. That is not to say that other characteristics are not good or even powerful. But if these powerful gifts and talents are not enough and we must have charity for sufficiency, what is charity? Several biblical passages address this question, but in the verses that follow, Paul provides an excellent overview of what charity looks like:

> *"Charity suffereth long, and is kind; charity envieth not; charity vaunteth not itself, is not puffed up, doth not behave itself unseemly; seeketh not her own, is not easily provoked, thinketh no evil; rejoiceth not in iniquity, but rejoiceth in the truth; beareth all things, believeth all things, hopeth all things, endureth all things. Charity never faileth; but whether there be prophesies, they shall fail; whether there be tongues, they shall cease; whether there be knowledge, it shall vanish away. For we know in part, and we prophesy in part. But when that which is perfect is come, then that which is in part shall be done away. When I was a child, I spake as a child, I understood as a child, I thought as a child: but when I became a man, I put away childish things. For now we see through a glass, darkly; but then face to face: now I know in part; but then shall I know even as also I am known. And now abideth faith, hope, charity; these three; but the greatest of these is charity."*
> *-I Corinthians 13:4-13*

The characteristics of charity are clearly delineated in the above passages. One of the distinguishing characteristics Paul points to is that charity will never fail but will endure always. The other gifts are important, but they have limited and temporary application. Charity, on the other hand, is eternal.

> *"Remember when you leave this earth, you can take with you nothing that you have received, only what you have*

*given: a heart enriched by honest service and love, sacrifice
and courage."*
-St. Francis of Assisi

*"I have held many things in my hand, and I have lost
them all, but whatever I have placed in God's hands, that
I still possess."*
-Corrie Ten Boom

While Paul provides the universal description of charity, we are
provided with a succinct and powerful "name" for charity. The prophet
Moroni writes:

*"…charity is the pure love of Christ, and it endureth
forever."*
-Book of Mormon, Moroni 7:47

Joy is tied to charity and service, but not to service that is mechan-
ically exercised. It must be driven by caring and compassion. This
amounts to saying that it must be driven by the pure love of Christ.
In addition to the passages describing the concept of charity above,
other verses of the Bible further define this central concept:

"Let all your things be done with charity."
-I Corinthians 16:14

*"And above all these things put on charity, which is the
bond of perfectness."*
-Colossians 3:14

"Now the end of the commandment is charity out of a pure heart, and of a good conscience, and of faith, unfeigned."
-1 Timothy 1:5

"And above all things have fervent charity among your-selves: for charity shall cover the multitude of sins."
-1 Peter 4:8

How many times have we thought ill of someone and then watched that person commit an act of charity? The thought then enters the mind and heart that they can't be all bad. Charity is a great healer.

Charity is benevolent giving with no expectation of return. Love Him and His children by looking outward to the needs of others and we find joy in our lives. Some have described it as a light that shines when we commit an act of charity. Something of an apocryphal story that has circulated for years tells a tale of selflessness and charity:

"A little girl was critically ill. She needed a special kind of blood for a transfusion to save her life. Her brother had the same type of blood. The doctors asked him if he would be willing to give his blood so his sister might live. Without hesitating, the young boy said, "Sure!" After the blood transfusion was completed, the brother turned to the doctor and asked softly, "Now, sir, when do I die?" It took only a moment for the doctor to realize the young boy had thought that giving blood to his sister would kill him. But he was willing to die for her."
-The Friend Magazine, February 1974

ANN MARGRET

Another such story of charity comes from a friend's Facebook post:

"Richard (my husband) never really talked a lot about his time in Vietnam, other than [that] he had been shot by a sniper. However, he had a rather grainy 8x10 black and white photo he had taken at a USO show of Ann Margret with Bob Hope in the background that was one of his treasures.

A few years ago, Ann Margret was doing a book signing at a local bookstore. Richard wanted to see if he could get her to sign the treasured photo, so he arrived at the bookstore at 12 o'clock for the 7:30 p.m. signing.

When I got there after work, the line went all the way around the bookstore, circled the parking lot, and disappeared behind the parking garage. Before her appearance, bookstore employees announced that she would only sign her book and no memorabilia would be permitted.

Richard was disappointed, but wanted to show her the photo and let her know how much those shows meant to

*lonely GI's so far from home. Ann Margret came out look-
ing as beautiful as ever, and, as second in line, it was soon
Richard's turn.*

*He presented the book for her signature and then took
out the photo. When he did, there were many shouts from
the employees that she would not sign it. Richard said, 'I
understand. I just wanted her to see it.' She took one look
at the photo, tears welled up in her eyes and she said, 'This
is one of my gentlemen from Vietnam and I most certainly
will sign his photo. I know what these men did for their
country and I always have time for 'my gentlemen.'" With
that, she pulled Richard across the table and planted a big
kiss on him. She then made quite a to-do about the brav-
ery of the young men she met over the years, how much
she admired them, and how much she appreciated them.
There weren't too many dry eyes among those close enough
to hear. She then posed for pictures and acted as if he were
the only one there. That night was a turning point for
him. He walked a little straighter and, for the first time
in years, was proud to be a Vet. I will never forget Ann
Margret for her graciousness and how much that small act
of kindness meant to my husband.*

*Later at dinner Richard was very quiet when I asked if
he'd like to talk about it My big, strong husband broke
down in tears. 'That's the first time anyone ever thanked
me for my time in the Army,' he said.*

*I now make it a point to say 'Thank you' to every person I
come across who served in our armed forces. Freedom does*

not come cheap, and I am grateful for all those who have served their country."

THE CONTRACT

Charity is the fundamental principle in all this talk of joy. As we serve others through charity, we come to joy. We have, what you might call, a unilateral contract with God who has said that when we love one another, we will be rewarded with joy. I learned about bilateral and unilateral contracts in law school many decades ago now. From what I remember, a bilateral contract is a promise in exchange for a promise, mutually obligating the parties to perform. A unilateral contract, by contrast, is a promise for an act. If the act is not performed, the promisor is not obligated to fulfil the promise. If we serve others, then God blesses us with joy. It is an open-ended offer from God in exchange for an act of charity from us. This includes both immediate blessings of peace in this life and unimaginable gifts to come in the next. There are no time limits for performance on our part to receive the benefit of God's bargain with us. No matter what our prior acts or positions in life may have been, if we commit charity we call upon God's gift of joy.

> *"But learn that he who doeth the works of righteousness shall receive his reward even peace in this world, and eternal life in the world to come."*
> -Doctrine and Covenants 59:23

THE CONNECTION

There are times and events in life that change us, that make us susceptible to new thoughts or ideas, that can make us change the direction of our view of life. One such event occurred to me that formed the basis for many of the thoughts and ideas set forth in the pages of this book.

On September 2, 1991, my nephew, Thomas Bryce Palfreyman was born to my brother Thomas and his sweet wife, Darla Shumway Palfreyman. It was immediately apparent that he was born with a small but serious hole in his heart and a hernia that was described to me by my mother as "crossing almost his entire body." I was asked to give a blessing to Bryce that would hopefully help his condition so that he could be healed. My religion believes in prayer to help heal emotional stresses and/or physical ills.

My father and I drove from South Pasadena, California to Diamond Bar, California, approximately 45 minutes away. On the way out we talked about all kinds of things from Lakers Basketball to the state of politics, and briefly, Bryce's condition. We were met at the hospital by Tom who brought us up to speed on Bryce's heart issue and his hernia. My father consecrated little Bryce's head with a drop of oil in preparation for the receiving of a blessing, meaning that he pronounced a prayer asking for the Lord's guidance in what pronouncements the prayer might include. I then put my hands (fingers, more accurately) on Bryce's little head, sealed the consecration, and commenced with a blessing that I will never forget. I went to the hospital to give Bryce a blessing of healing so that the hole in his heart would close and his hernia could be successfully repaired. That is not at all what happened.

I began speaking but then almost immediately became something of a bystander as words continued from my mouth but not from my mind. The words to Bryce were spoken as if he could fully understand everything that was being said to him. It was as if I was just a third-party observer to a conversation between Bryce and some unseen being. I felt as if the veil between heaven and earth had been pierced, and Bryce was being spoken to by someone from the realm he had just come from, someone who knew him. Remember, Bryce was just a day or two old at the time of this blessing.

Bryce was told that he would not get better and that he would never be healthy. The message went on to tell him that his life would be filled with physical trials and that it would be so bad going forward that God would embrace him now if he determined to give up his earthly life and return to his home in heaven. If he did that, he would have fulfilled all of the obligations that he had come to this world to fulfill.

On the other hand, this voice went on to tell Bryce that the other option was to stay in this world and live through all the physical and emotional trials and tribulations that would beset him. By staying and enduring these trials, he would be providing his parents, his extended family, friends, and even strangers opportunities to serve and thereby feel joy in their lives.

These words were closed out by sharing that either way, God would accept his decision and embrace him whether it was immediately or after he had fulfilled a lifetime sojourn on earth. The decision to live or die was left entirely in Bryce's hands.

At the conclusion of the blessing, I really could not look at Tom. These were words that I certainly did not rehearse and did not fully appreciate or comprehend at the time. I really did not know how to explain what had just happened.

Some term these kinds of inexplicable events as out-of-body experiences, as if to explain the other-worldly nature of the feeling. A Book of Mormon prophet tried to explain it:

> *"Now when I think of the success of these my brethern my*
> *soul is carried away, even to the separation of it from the*
> *body as it were, so great is my joy."*
> *-Alma 29:16*

What I knew was that I had not provided any hope that Bryce would get better. I slowly backed out of the hospital room and started sheepishly walking down the hall. Tom came after me and when he caught up with me in the hallway, he asked what I thought the blessing meant. All I could say was that whether Bryce lived or died, it was all up to Bryce, that he understood the decision he was making even at two days old. My understanding of the veil between our world and the pre-existent world was dramatically altered and shaped by this blessing. The veil is thin, very real, and very thin. And at times, there are those who pass through that veil. I witnessed it on this almost miraculous occasion.

On the drive home, we got to about Monrovia, just over half the drive, before either my father or I said anything. The silence was broken when my father, like Tom before, inquired as to what I thought the blessing meant. I responded by asking him about Bryce's condition. I asked if the hole in the heart and the hernia were all that they knew about? He said yes, looking very concerned by the question. I told my father that those issues were the least of Bryce's problems going forward and that he would never be fully functional. That was the end of our brief conversation, and we concluded the drive home in complete silence.

Bryce lived, and through the years, he influenced literally thousands of people's lives for the good. Tom and Darla, Carly (Bryce's sister), his brothers, friends, teachers, caregivers, neighbors, and members of the church congregations that Tom and Darla belonged to, all participated in seeing to Bryce's needs. All participants in Bryce's life looked outward toward Bryce. There was no thought of what Bryce could do for them. In doing so, their cares and challenges were briefly set aside as they served him. Joy in service to Bryce replaced worldly cares.

Tom and Darla spent a lifetime selflessly caring for their son. Their daughter, Carly, was virtually a perfect sibling. Bryce's little brothers, Grayson and Elijah, were loving brothers. Members of Bryce's various congregations celebrated the opportunity to help with his care. Caretakers throughout the years who had worked with Bryce expressed gratitude for what Bryce had taught them before leaving this earthly life. Charitable service had brought joy. Bryce had somehow agreed to be the vehicle for joy.

A specific example may help to show how all of this worked. As Bryce grew in stature, he became too large for Darla to get him in and out of the family vehicle. It meant that special trips, like going to the doctor, became very difficult. Routine trips, like going to church, became almost impossible. Tom and Darla needed to upgrade the family vehicle to a wheelchair accessible van with a lift. But that was not within their budget.

One night, their bishop called and asked them to come to see him at the church house. When they arrived, the bishop announced that a family in the congregation would pay for a wheelchair lift to be installed in their van so that they could move Bryce around more easily. When they asked who contributed the miracle gift, the bishop relayed that the family making the gift wanted to remain anonymous and that Tom and Darla should consider the gift as coming from the entire congregation as everyone in the congregation would have made the gift if they had the means. Joy was a result for the givers, for the bishop, and for Tom and Darla. Tom and Darla had many of these experiences over the years because Bryce chose to live.

At his funeral, somewhere in the neighborhood of one thousand people appeared to celebrate Bryce's life and the lessons of service that Bryce had taught us all. One of his last caretakers knelt at his coffin and held Bryce's hand. She would not let go. Tears streamed down her cheeks. Her service to Bryce had brought meaning to her life and true joy to her soul. She may not have fully understood God's promise of joy through service or how it all worked. But she was keenly aware of her connection to Bryce and the joy that she felt. She did not need to fully understand the unilateral contract of God's promise for her act. But she lived it, and it was real to her. At Bryce's funeral, we were all comforted in the hope and believe that Bryce fulfilled his mission and had chosen his own time to leave this worldly existence.

The whole event that was Bryce's life has caused me to reflect on our trajectory of existence, where we came from, why we are here, and where we go when we lay aside our physical bodies. I do not pretend to know specific answers to many of these almost imponderable questions. But God lives and loves us. He knows us and wants for each of us to be joyful. He has provided a way. We exist to serve each other, to help each other. Caring, compassion, and charity are the tools that place us on the true pathway to a full life of joy, no matter what obstacles beset us.

Bryce never walked, he was never able to speak with any real clarity, he could not eat solid food and spent much of his life in bed. He went through many surgeries and hospitalizations before passing away at age 25. He was what some would refer to as a burden. They would be wrong. He was a hero. He was not a burden to his family, friends, and service providers. Instead, he was their vehicle for service…for joy.

As an aside, Tom and I did not speak about the blessing that was pronounced in that hospital room in Diamond Bar, California for many years. When he finally did feel comfortable enough to bring it up, Tom shared with me a blessing that he had given to Darla, his wife, on the morning of the same day that Bryce was born. In that blessing, he told Darla that Bryce would be the greatest challenge of her life and that she should trust God and endure. Tom had no idea what that blessing really meant. Neither he nor Darla had any prior knowledge of any health issues that Bryce would have. Tom has articulated that the delivery of the content of his blessing to Darla was much the same as when I blessed Bryce. It was as if he was a conduit for the transmission of a message that was not his.

Darla's life was dramatically altered as she committed to Bryce's care. She served on a daily basis. Changing diapers, feedings, doctors' appointments, monitoring medications, and sleepless nights all seemed daunting. At times, joy was not what Darla was thinking about. But in the end, Bryce taught Darla about service and joy.

He had brought joy into the world by virtue of his very existence, and he had willingly sacrificed his own comfort so that so many could serve and obtain joy in that service. The service that Bryce provided in this world was truly a grand gesture and sacrifice on his part. For most of us, the outward service opportunities that come our way are much more manageable but can be just as rewarding.

King Benjamin in the Book of Mormon taught:

"…that when ye are in the service of your fellow beings ye are only in the service of your God."
-Mosiah 2:17

Within the framework of the sacrificial outward looking work of Jesus Christ, the responsibility for our joy in this life is our own. One of the paradoxes of Christianity is that in order to bring about heaven here and now in this world for each of us, we need to learn how to put the needs and the lives of others before our own:

> *"Then said Jesus unto his disciples, If any man will come after me, let him deny himself, and take up his cross, and follow me. For whosoever will save his life shall lose it: and whosoever will lose his life for my sake shall find it.*
>
> *For what is a man profited, if he shall gain the whole world, and lose his own soul? Or what shall a man give in exchange for his soul? For the Son of man shall come in the glory of his father with his angels; and then he shall reward every man according to his works."*
> -Matthew 16:24-27

God has offered up a unilateral contract to all of us. He has promised us joy as our reward for charitable acts of service to others.

PAUL AND BETTY

President Paul and Sister Betty Morris were much like surrogate parents for me during my "Two Years in God's Mormon Army" (what I call my time as a Mormon missionary). I spent two years away from everyone and almost everything I had known in my life during my mission for The Church of Jesus Christ of Latter-day Saints in Bangkok, Thailand. Once my missionary service was complete, I had very little contact with the Morris family for years. This was not by choice but rather as a result of the simple course of life, geographical distance, and poor prioritizing on my part.

Some 30 years later, I received a telephone call from John Montgomery, one of my missionary companions, wherein he related to me that Betty Morris had called him with the sad news that Paul was suffering from pulmonary fibrosis. She asked if it would be possible for four of us, who served together in Thailand, to come to the Morris home in Vancouver, Washington, to do a little yard work that Paul had become anxious about but could no longer do.

At the time, I was living in Laguna Beach, California. My three other comrades were at the time living in the San Francisco Bay area, San Diego, and Utah. Betty asked that we come that next weekend. Normally, I would respond that I was quite busy with work, coaching my children in various sports, and unsuccessfully doing my own yard work. But I cared deeply for the Morris family and the close connection

I had with them through the course of my missionary work. I had a difficult time thinking of Paul Morris being ill. The decision as to whether or not to go to Washington was surprisingly simple, and I chose the charitable thing and decided to make time to go to the Morris's home, despite short notice and other duties that would have to be placed on hold. The four of us made our plans and we went.

That Friday, Roger Pace, Steve Welling, John Montgomery, and I met up in Portland, Oregon and drove across the Columbia River into Vancouver and then on to the Morris home. We almost immediately forgot why we were there, and instead, we began our own missionary reunion of sorts. Arriving at the Morris' home, the reunion continued now with Betty joining us. (Paul had gone to bed.)

In the morning, we had breakfast with the Morris family and then went out to assess our chores for the day. Paul's yard was in great shape, better than any of ours, we quickly concluded. But then, that in fact was Paul. He was always meticulous in all things that we had ever observed him doing. We did find a couple of things to do and made a list of supplies that we would need at Home Depot. The day went almost perfectly. John supervised, Roger measured, Steve did the saw work, and I did the digging since I had no other particularly useful skills. Paul would come out to the back patio periodically and sit with his oxygen tank and quietly visit with us. We all filled each other in on our lives and families since our missionary days.

As the day wore on, we slowly came to realize that we were not spending time in Vancouver, Washington to do yard work at all. We came to rekindle relationships that were important to a dying man— an arrangement set up by a truly caring and compassionate wife. It was an almost perfect day. In fact, it was perfect. Betty Morris really didn't care about the yard. She cared about her husband…and about us. She had brought us together in order to reconnect and share a few of life's most wonderful moments.

It was akin to a spiritual weekend retreat for all of us. Our lives had all gone in different directions, and yet we were still very close, having shared two years in the mostly selfless service to others in Thailand. We were able to spend quiet time with a man that we all highly respected and loved. The stories of his life filled our minds and hearts connecting all of us closer than we had ever been before. Things got even better on Sunday morning. The four of us went to church with Betty where we were introduced as four of her missionary sons. Sunday afternoon we exchanged missionary stories. As missionaries we were privy to missionary capers that nobody ever wanted the Mission President to know about. On this day, he was regaled with many stories about 19-year-old boys trying, sometimes unsuccessfully, to live lives of service while at the same time periodically falling back into the foibles of 19-year-old boys. Amazingly, he was more aware of some of our stories than we had supposed.

Paul and Betty then filled in some of the details of stories that we had only heard rumors about. Time stood still for us. Paul's illness, our worldly concerns, all had long disappeared from our minds. We were enthralled with the goodness of the moment. The charity (pure love of God) that flowed in those moments ushered us into a world of joy.

Monday morning came all too soon, and we were back to our own worlds with all the accompanying problems of life. But we had all been filed with a joyous remembrance of the goodness of life.

Then, the next morning we got the call. President Morris had passed away. Since then, I have tried never to pass on opportunities to render compassionate service. I now work to attend weddings, funerals and other consequential events in family and/or friends' lives. The resulting act of charity is the consideration for God's blessings of joy in my life.

SERMON ON THE MOUNT

The next question is: "Whose needs do we put ahead of our own?" Jesus taught that lesson clearly in the famous story of The Good Samaritan:

> "And, behold a certain lawyer stood up, and tempted him, saying, Master, what shall I do to inherit eternal life? He said unto him, What is written in the law? How readest thou? And he answering said, Thou shalt love the Lord thy God with all thy heart, and with all thy soul, and with all thy strength, and with all thy mind; and thy neighbor as thyself. And he said unto him, Thou hast answered right: this do, and thou shalt live. But he, willing to justify himself, said unto Jesus, and who is my neighbor? And Jesus answering said, A certain man went down from Jerusalem to Jericho, and fell among thieves, which stripped him of his raiment, and wounded him, and departed, leaving him half dead. And by chance there came down a certain priest that way: and when he saw him, he passed by on the other side. And likewise a Levite, when he was at the place, came and looked on him, and passed by on the other side. But a certain Samaritan, as he journeyed, came where he was: and when he saw him,

*he had compassion on him, and went to him, and bound
up his wounds, pouring in oil and wine, and set him
on his own beast, and brought him to an inn, and took
care of him. And on the morrow when he departed, he
took out two pence, and gave them to the host, and said
unto him, take care of him: and whatsoever thou spendest
more, when I come again, I will repay thee. Which now of
these three, thinkest thou, was neighbor unto him that fell
among the thieves? And he said, he that shewed mercy on
him. Then said Jesus unto him, Go, and do thou likewise."*
-Luke 10: 25-37

The Sermon on the Mount teaches us to put others' needs ahead of our own. It does not matter what religion, race, color, creed, gender, sexual identity, or nationality anyone is. We are all children of God. As we serve, God will see to our needs better then we could address our needs on our own. Our lives will then be filled with joy.

*"This is the true joy in life, the being used for a purpose
recognized by yourself as a mighty one, the being a force of
nature, instead of a selfish, feverish little clod of ailments
and grievances complaining that the world will not devote
itself to making you happy. I am of the opinion that my
life belongs to the whole community, and it is my privilege
to do for it whatever I can. I want to be thoroughly used
up when I die, for the harder I work, the more I live. I
rejoice in life for its own sake. Life is no brief candle to
me, it is a sort of splendid torch which I've got a hold of
for the moment, and I want to make it burn as brightly as
possible before handing it onto the future generation."*
-George Bernard Shaw

Joy is knowing and realizing one's purpose in the world. That purpose is to care for our brothers and sisters of every stripe.

"The purpose of life is not to be happy. It is to be useful, to be honorable, to be compassionate, to have it make some difference that you have lived and lived well."
-Ralph Waldo Emerson

To get to joy we need to place our own interests in a secondary position to our neighbors. The Dalai Lama boils it all down to:

"We are but visitors on this planet. We are here for ninety or one hundred years at the very most. During that period, we must try to do something useful with our lives. If you contribute to other people's happiness, you will find the true goal, the true meaning of life."

He then says on another occasion:

"This is my simple religion. There is no need for temples; no need for complicated philosophy. Our own brain, our own heart is our temple; philosophy is kindness."

"Service to others is the rent you pay for your room here on earth."
-Mohammad Ali

Caring, compassion, and charity can bind all mankind together in various expressions of love. Political and religious differences, disparities in wealth, and all other differences can all cohabit, mingle, and arrive at joy by caring, showing compassion, and committing charity without judgement.

*"Kindness and love are the most curative herbs and agents
in human intercourse."*
-Friedrich Nietzsche

Picture a quiver holding three arrows: the quiver representing love and the arrows representing various manifestations of love. The arrows are caring, compassion, and charity. Together they comprise the THREE C'S OF JOY.

In very simple terms the golden rule applies here:

"Do unto others as you would have them do onto you."
-Matthew 7:12

The suffering and needs of others are the targets of those arrows in our quiver of love. Note that these arrows point outward toward others. Looking outward, serving the needs of others, is the pathway to joy. Pointing your arrows toward yourself is difficult, impractical, and rather foolish. Inward focus may provide you with some measure of happiness, but joy requires outward reach. Lifting the burdens of others by relieving their pain and suffering allows us to move away from our own suffering, providing us with a calm mind.

There is a practical impact to our own personal situations as we turn toward the needs of others:

*"The body heals with play, the mind heals with laughter,
and spirit heals with joy."*
-Old Proverb

A calm mind paints a beautiful image of peace and tranquility. Jesus makes a similar comment by way of a promise:

"But the Comforter, which is the Holy Ghost, whom the father will send in my name, he shall teach you all things, and bring all things to your remembrance, whatsoever I have said unto you. Peace I leave with you, my peace I give unto you: not as the world giveth, give I unto you. Let not your heart be troubled, neither let it be afraid."
-John 14:26-27

Worldly peace was not the object of this promise. Inner peace, leading to joy was the reference and the promise. Regardless of our circumstances in a worldly sense, joy is possible. Love your fellow beings through service. Joy is the reward regardless of other circumstances.

As we take each arrow out of the quiver, the direction in which we point the arrow makes all the difference between happiness and joy. It has nothing at all to do with degree—it is about <u>direction</u>. It has everything to do with our motivation and where we focus our attention. As we point our arrows of love in the direction of those around us, we truly can expect to obtain joy.

A very popular motivational guru puts it this way:

"You can have everything in life you want if you will just help enough other people get what they want."
-Zig Ziglar

MARRIAGE

Now apply that distinct difference in the direction of our arrows/ focus to the institution of marriage, a relationship that seems to have lost some of its luster. It is said that for marriages to work, each partner has to be willing to meet the other halfway. With that attitude, the divorce rate hovers just under 50 percent (PolitiFact.com, January 28, 2021). What would happen to that divorce rate if we consistently applied the idea that joy comes from putting the needs of our spouse first? If each side in a marriage put the needs of the other first, 100 percent of the time, each would be blessed with joy rather than constant disappointment with unfulfilled expectations for happiness. If we are constantly kind to our partners with no expectation of anything in return, then we would rarely be disappointed and our partners would always feel love. Where would the divorce rate go then?

When we date, it seems that we are better at caring about what makes our dating partner happy. For some reason, time goes by and we tend to diminish our efforts to please each other and replace those efforts with worrying about our own needs. Malaise sets in and the question arises, "what's in it for me?" As we turn our focus inward, the relationship suffers. The fix is to refocus our arrows of caring, compassion, and charity directly towards our mate. Joy then returns as a possibility.

*"Carry out random acts of kindness, with no expectation
of reward, safe in the knowledge that one day someone
might do the same for you."*
-Princess Diana

Clearly, marriage relationships would improve dramatically if the simple principle of charity was the engine driving each side of a marital partnership. The Bible relates:

*"Let nothing be done through strife or vain glory: but in
lowliness of mind let each esteem the other better than
themselves."*
-Philippians 2:3

In the secular world, we all seem to be pretty wrapped up in "the pursuit of happiness." Thomas Jefferson thought so highly of happiness that he included it in the specifically identified God given rights in the Declaration of Independence, third only to life and liberty. For some, travel is an elixir. Others hike, ski, play sports, work out, quilt, eat out; you name it. There is an almost endless range of choices of activities that can make us happy. We all seem to crave something that makes us happy.

For me, there was a time when I could play basketball all day. For Claralyn and I, our annual Dodger baseball games with Steve and Jane Bradford, including open and engaging conversations and the perfect Dodger hot dogs, were definitely happy times. I think it's important to note here that time with others is not necessarily self-serving or inwardly focused. The best times are had when we share joy. Speaking broadly for society as a whole, we hope that everyone around us can find their own happiness. We have hundreds of choices for activities that lead us to happiness. What they all have in common is that they all look to satisfy our inward interests. We are looking to make ourselves happy. Our attention is directed inward, not outward toward others.

In a secular world, that kind of self-interest is deemed just fine. It admittedly provides a measure of happiness. In a more spiritually-oriented world, it is not fine standing alone, as it does not see to the needs of others and therefore leads us away from joy. Happiness and joy are not always mutually exclusive. But not being aware of the difference may rob us of the gift of either.

> *"As you grow older, you will discover that you have two hands; one for helping yourself, and the other for helping others."*
> -Audrey Hepburn

ORGANIZED RELIGION

In recent times, organized religion has taken a beating, sometimes for very legitimate reasons. Overbearing judgments by religious leaders, arrogance, hypocrisy, and misbehavior on the part of religious leaders have all given organized religion a black eye. Many ask, "Why should I be involved with a religion that…(fill in your own complaint)?"

One of the reasons, and I think the biggest one, for participating in organized religion is that it provides us with opportunities to serve within a community, whatever religious community that happens to be. While churches are not the only organizations providing service opportunities, they do provide a spiritual context for those services. As we act and react within that community, opportunities to serve become more easily recognizable. Service opportunities arise on a regular basis.

There are times when we can provide strength to others. There are also times when others can provide strength to us. It creates a wellspring of readymade service opportunities in, hopefully, some kind of organized fashion. It creates a wonderfully synergistic opportunity and atmosphere in which to participate in generating joy through service.

"To get the full value of joy you must have someone to divide it with."
-Mark Twain

TRACTION

Our oldest daughter, Claire, was five years old, and we had two younger daughters at the time. Claire was in the backyard jumping over a large pickle jar. Each time she jumped off the step and over the pickle jar, she would move the pickle jar a little farther out just to see how far she could jump. Unfortunately, she found out, landing on the pickle jar and falling backwards on her arm. The arm snapped and she had to go to the hospital immediately. She had broken her elbow in several places, and the doctors advised my wife that she would have to be placed in traction with pins through her elbow for a period of two weeks in order for the bones to heal in a way that would give her an opportunity to possibly have full use of her arm. It was quite frightening.

I was called at work and told of the terrifying events of the day. I treated my Oldsmobile Cutlass Supreme as some kind of Formula One race car making full use of the emergency parking lanes on the 170 and 110 freeways to try to get through the downtown Los Angeles rush hour traffic and over to the Huntington Memorial Hospital in Pasadena to get to my daughter. I was somewhat beside myself.

When I ran into Claire's hospital room, I was met by both of her grandfathers who had just finished praying with Claire that she would heal and that she would have full use of her arm without any residual problems. When I looked at my little girl, she was already pinned with her arm hanging in a sling, a position that she would have to remain in over the next two weeks. But she was smiling with her two grandfathers having stepped in to provide sublime comfort.

I stayed with Claire that night and by the middle of the next morning our congregation's women's leader had put together a two-week calendar divided into one-hour increments. By the end of the day, that entire calendar was filled with the names of friends, family, and members of our congregation. All took turns sitting with Claire, coloring with Claire, reading to Claire, singing with Claire, sleeping in Claire's room overnight and generally making sure that she was never left alone. In the end, her two-week stay in the hospital required her to be alone no more than 10 minutes. Claire loved it. Who wouldn't love that much attention? There was such an outpouring of caring, compassion, and charity that the hardship of being in traction for two weeks became a blessing that brought people together in service. The joy that came out of that event far outweighed the injury and heartache that accompanied it.

The concept of outward service as the source of joy is beautifully analogized by Pope Francis:

> *"Rivers do not drink their own water; Trees do not eat their own fruit; The sun does not shine on itself and flowers do not spread their fragrance for themselves. Living for others is a rule of nature. We are all born to help each other. No matter how difficult it is…Life is good when you are happy; but much better when others are happy because of you."*

Jackie Robinson, the great Brooklyn Dodger and the first Black Major League Baseball player, put it in plain terms this way:

"Life is not important except in the impact that it has on other lives."

Jackie Robinson states clearly that life in isolation is unimportant. The things we do, if they only impact ourselves, have no real significance. What is important is not what benefits us, but the impact our actions have on others. We are more than the sum of our own actions, as our actions help to create the world around us. Our actions can actually create joy. Too often, we judge ourselves by what we have accomplished for ourselves. We may not put it in those terms, but, as Jackie Robinson teaches, the question has to be turned around: what beneficial impact have our lives, actions, and words had on others' lives? The answer to that question relates directly to joy.

Sir Richard Branson even applied this same kind of service-oriented thinking to business:

"If you aren't making a difference in other people's lives, you shouldn't be in business. It's that simple."

What distinguishes a happy life from a joyous life is our ability to see beyond our own wants and desires, reaching out to connect with those around us by seeing their needs and that we can help them to meet these needs. This is caring. From there we can then perceive how to help. This is compassion. Finally, charity consists of a willingness to act for the benefit of others. Together all of this is nothing more than simple kindness. Kindness brings joy.

OFFLOADING SERVICE

In the secular world, we generally fall into the trap of offloading the need to serve by hoping some charitable organization will do the good deeds for us or by seeking governmental action to attend to the needs of others, hence, compelling behavior of the individual only by way of taxes or regulations. Charity by charitable organizations or by governmental fiat is well intended to make sure that everyone is cared for. However, the separation from our own charitable actions and the impact on the recipient, diminishes our capacity to achieve joy because we are no longer directly involved.

Hopefully by contrast, religious charity operations require voluntary and personal efforts, and come from individual participation. Since it is personal, it tends to be more direct and heartfelt. It also tends to connect us to joy.

> *"The rights of man come not from the generosity of the state, but from the hand of God."*
> -John F. Kennedy

This shows up particularly in the political arena. John F. Kennedy tried to move the secular world's contemplated pursuit of happiness (through taxes and regulations) toward the spiritual approach that connects us to actions of service which provides a greater opportunity to obtain joy. In his January 20, 1961 Inaugural Address, President Kennedy famously said:

"Ask not what your country can do for you, ask what you can do for your country."

The Peace Corps developed from that attitude and has brought good to the world ever since with volunteers connecting their acts of service to those in need, thereby providing an avenue to achieve joy. But even outside the Peace Corps, those words have inspired millions of Americans to live their lives in a way that is focused not on what they can get, but on what they can contribute.

GOD

God, does He exist and if He does, how can He let so much evil happen? This question is referred to as "The Theodicy" and has been debated for thousands of years. If God is all powerful and all loving, how can there be evil? The answer seems to speak to the heart of many of the controversies in life. Would God compel not only behavior but also outcomes? Or is it that God has provided us with agency to choose between good and evil or even good, better, or best? Must God compel us in all things or do we learn by making our choices and living with the consequences? Would joy exist without choices?

> *"There are moments when I wish I could roll back the clock and take all the sadness away, but I have the feeling that if I did, the joy would be gone as well."*
> -Nicholas Sparks, *A Walk to Remember*

Would joy exist without hardships, challenges, and sadness?

> *"Some of you say, 'Joy is greater than sorrow', and others say, 'Ney, sorrow is greater', but I say unto you, they are inseparable. Together they come, and when one sits alone with you at your board, remember that the other is asleep on your bed."*
> -Kahlil Gibran, *The Prophet*

Our only real assets in life are our time, our agency, and our relationships. Agency is our ability to appraise, react, and choose. We have our agency to use our time in the manner that we see fit. God is the holder of all else. With this in mind, the test of the direction of our focus is quite simple. We will see who we really are when we see how our time and efforts are focused. We are defined by what we spend our time doing. How much of our caring, compassion, and charity gets used in our lives for the service of those around us? That's the only judgment we need to make.

I have learned, sometimes despite myself, that as I did the right things for the right reasons, I was rewarded with the joy that comes from God, a joy that lasts. I have also learned that when I make the selfish choice, joy escapes me and I am left with, at most, just happy. It seems to be a daily challenge to choose outward focus toward others over selfish desires. It is far more satisfying to connect with others through service than to pursue any state of happiness that I achieve on my own. Sometimes this joy is described as light.

It seems that agency, or the ability to choose between one thing or another, provides not only a learning experience but also a point of reference to recognize joy and opportunities to experience joy when relieving the evil or misfortune that has beset others. If sorrow was never part of life, then joy could never be fully felt or understood:

> *"For it must needs be, that there is an opposition in all things. If not so, my firstborn in the wilderness, righteousness could not be brought to pass, neither wickedness, neither holiness nor misery, neither good nor bad. Wherefore, all things must needs be a compound in one; wherefore, if it should be one body it must needs remain as dead, having no life neither death, nor corruption nor incorruption, happiness nor misery, neither sense nor insensibility…wherefore, men are free according to the*

flesh; and all things are given them which are expedient unto man. And they are free to choose liberty and eternal life, through the great Mediator of all men, or to choose captivity and death, according to the captivity and power of the devil; for he seeketh that all men might be miserable like unto himself."
-2 Nephi 2:11, 27

Put another way:

"If a thing is free to be good it is also free to be bad. And free will is what made evil possible. Why, then, did God give them free will? Because free will, though it makes evil possible, is also the only thing that makes possible any love or goodness or joy worth having."
-C.S. Lewis, *Mere Christianity*

Where we are free to choose, we can make mistakes. The consequences follow and they are not always good. Hence, with poor choices, pain, suffering, and sorrow come into our lives. In what often seems unfair, one's own bad choices can cause pain in someone else's life as well. We are often required to suffer from the consequences of our own bad choices and from the bad choices of others. It is not God's will that people suffer. It is God's will that we choose correctly to feel of His joy rather than choosing incorrectly and feeling the adverse consequences of poor choices.

Our lives can present us with wonderful opportunities for learning how to obtain joy. We can choose to focus on our own narrow pursuits and interests, constantly falling just short of our own expectations, or we can learn to look outward to the needs of others and find joy in the process.

*"I am like a huge rough stone...and the only polishing I get
is when some corner gets rubbed off by coming in contact
with something else, striking with accelerated force...thus
I will become a smooth and polished shaft in the quiver of
the Almightly."*
-Joseph Smith Jr.

The difference between hardship and learning is perception and reaction. With each challenge we meet, we can either learn from it or be crushed by it. Learn joy.

THINGS WE LOVE

In some cases, we become attached to habits or riches and the things we can get with them. They become tied to our self-identity. In the case of Jesus Christ and the rich man, the rich man was sad because he appeared to be attached to his riches and he was made keenly aware of it by the challenge Jesus laid before him. He could not give his riches up. This focus on his riches and his attachment to them was the problem. It was the impediment to the rich man's moving into a world of joy.

In answer to the question from a lawyer about which was the great commandment, Jesus said:

> *"…Thou shalt love the Lord thy God with all thy heart, and with all thy soul, and with all thy mind. This is the first and great commandment. And the second is like unto it, Thou shalt love thy neighbor as thyself. On these two commandments hang all the law and the prophets."*
> *-Matthew 22:37-40*

The two great commandments Jesus highlights here do not deal with any of the "don'ts" of the law. For example, we are not told what activities to perform or avoid on Sunday. We are not told what is forbidden to eat or drink. The great commandments don't say anything about money. We are not asked to worry at all about our inward focus. Instead, the great commandments ask us to love God first and foremost. Interestingly then, we are not commanded to show that love directly to God. Instead, we are to show obedience to the first great commandment by complying with the second great commandment which is to love our neighbors. The direction of our attention is to be pointed toward the needs of others. It has been put another way:

> *"The Lord is first, my family and friends are second; and I am third."*
> -Gale Sayers in "I am Third"

By following this prioritization of outward focus of attention we gain significant side benefits that people often spend their lives seeking and never finding. There are so many lonely people in the world lamenting the lack of friends. It is almost like a dog chasing his tail and never reaching it. When we seek friends, it is hard to find them. When we seek ways to serve, friends abound:

> *"I sought my soul, but my soul I could not see. I sought my God, but my God eluded me. I sought my brother, and I found all three."*
> -William Blake

> *"If you go out looking for friends, you are going to find they are very scarce. If you go out to be a friend, you will find them everywhere."*
> -Zig Zigler

When our love and attention are pointed in the direction of ourselves, we are working toward creating our own happiness. That is short-lived and limited by our own talents and skills. That is the direction of the secular world and the rich man who Jesus invited to address the needs of others. In order to find a true joy, the direction of our minds and our hearts must point outwardly. That is how we show love and it constitutes our own pathway to joy. What all of this means is that in order to find lasting joy, we are required to put happiness into second place behind the needs of our fellow man.

> *"I don't know what your destiny will be, but one thing I know: the ones among you who will be really happy are those who have sought and found how to serve."*
> -Albert Switzer

> *"Life's most persistent and urgent question is 'What are you doing for others?'"*
> -Martin Luther King, Jr.

The Broadway play *Les Miserables* is one of my all-time favorite musicals. It tells of a man, Jean Val Jean, whose life progresses from one tragedy to another until he meets Cossette: a young girl he adopts and takes responsibility for. She takes his heart. He determines to care for her every need so that she does not experience the life that he lived. He becomes Cossette's surrogate father. He keeps her close at hand, always. Inevitably, Cossette falls in love with Marius, who ultimately needs to be saved by Jean Val Jean. Our hero prays for the life of Marius:

> *"God on high, hear my prayer, In my need, you have always been there, You can take, you can give, Let him be, let him live. If I die, let me die, let him live. Bring him home, bring him home."*

The beauty of the verse is that Jean Val Jean has offered up his own life in exchange for the happiness of the love of his life, Cossette. After a long life of turmoil and trouble, he has realized that his real joy comes from serving Cossette, not from thinking of his own hard life or selfish desire to keep Cossette close by his side. She is in love with Marius. Jean Val Jean must save Marius, not for his own self-interest (which, on the contrary, would be to get Marius out of the picture so that he would still have Cossette by his side), but to serve Cossette. So, he risks his life for Cossette by serving Marius. Joy follows.

> *"If ye keep my commandments, ye shall abide in my love;*
> *even as I have kept my Father's commandments, and abide*
> *in his love. These things have I spoken unto you, that my*
> *joy might remain in you, and that your joy might be full.*
> *This is my commandment, that ye love one another, as I*
> *have loved you."*
> *-John 15:10-13*

This commandment is later repeated in more concrete terms as follows:

> *"Bear ye one another's burdens, and so fulfill the law of*
> *Christ."*
> *-Galatians 6:2*

TRUST GOD

The problem that we face in even thinking about focusing our attention outward is, "Who will take care of us?" It feels like we are giving up the easier pursuit of happiness for the deeper pursuit of joy and that is frightening. When confidence in a higher, benevolent being doesn't exist, it is difficult (though not impossible) to even think of serving others. The secularists often turn toward government for comfort as a replacement for God. It is a question that has come up in the past and the answer has been given in no uncertain terms:

> *"Trust in the Lord with all thine heart; and lean not unto thine own understanding. In all thy ways acknowledge him, and he shall direct thy paths."*
> -Proverbs 3:5-6

> *"I have discovered that the people who believe most strongly in the next life do the most good in the present one."*
> -C.S. Lewis

In order to move from the realm of a self-absorbed pursuit of one's own happiness to the realm of selfless joy, it helps to trust in God. That seems to be a very difficult thing to do as illustrated by the following:

"I remember a story I heard once about a great man of faith who loved the Lord with all his heart and believed that his faith in God was one of his most valuable assets. One day while hiking near his home he slipped and fell and began sliding down the mountain to his certain death. At that crucial moment he reached out and grabbed a branch before plunging into the great abyss. As he hung there contemplating the inevitable, he lifted up a prayer to the Lord. 'God, please send someone to save me,' he said. 'I promise to serve you more and with greater zeal, please save me! I have faith that you will send someone.'

All at once he heard an audible voice that he knew could only be that of God himself. And the voice said, 'I will save you. Just let go of the branch.' There was a pause and then the man responded, 'What do you mean let go of the branch? If I do, surely I will die.' God replied, 'You said you have faith that I will save you, trust me and let go of the branch.' The moment of truth…how large is your faith?

It is easy to proclaim a deep faith in the Power of God, but how often are we asked to put that faith to the test and operate in it. I am in the place of great opportunity right now. It has required me to 'let go of the branch.'"
-Mary Tina on *Faith, Family and the Farm.* Jan. 26, 2011

As we distance ourselves from God, we lose hope in God's protective and providential blessings upon us. Abinadi was a missionary in the Book of Mormon. He trusted that so long as he was doing God's work, he would be protected. He was correct:

"And now when the king had heard these words, he said unto his priests: Away with this fellow, and slay him; for what have we to do with him, for he is mad. And they stood forth and attempted to lay their hands on him; but he withstood them, and said unto them: "Touch me not, for God shall smite you if ye lay your hands upon me, for I have not delivered the message which the Lord sent me to deliver; neither have I told you that which ye requested that I should tell; therefore, God will not suffer that I shall be destroyed at this time. But I must fulfill the commandments wherewith God has commanded me; and because I have told you the truth ye are angry with me. And again, because I have spoken the word of God ye have judged me that I am mad. Now it came to pass after Abinadi had spoken these words that the people of King Noah durst not lay their hands on him, for the Spirit of the Lord was upon him; and his face shone with exceeding luster, even as Moses' did while in the mount of Sinai, while speaking with the Lord."
-Mosiah 13:1-5

Trust in God's existence however you perceive it. The Founding Fathers of the United States had differing opinions about God, and therefore they went with Thomas Jefferson's term, "The Creator." Perceive God how you will. But trust that however you perceive Him, joy is His gift for caring, compassion and charity. Then feel the warmth of God's light.

"Why do we close our eyes when we pray, cry, kiss, or dream? Because the most beautiful things in life are not seen but felt by the heart."
-Denzel Washington

SHUTTING OUT GOD

In our secular world, we completely obliterate even the mention of God in our schools. The same often holds true in our lives generally with the popular refrain that we can talk about "anything but religion or politics." Our children are taught about everything except God. Without the ability to discuss God, how can we ever learn to trust in a God who is our actual source of joy? Knowing or at least having a belief or a hope that God provides joy in exchange for caring, compassion, and charity helps us through the brambles of life and toward the fruit that has been promised.

I have four daughters who have each acknowledged to me, in one way or another, that they had no idea about the depth of love that they could have for their children until their children were actually born. They can describe that depth of love, but they cannot prove it, except in their everyday activities by showing love for their children, which they do extraordinarily well. That depth of love between a mother and her child exists and is real even though it is not provable by any current scientific formula.

In the movie, *A Walk to Remember,* God was compared to the wind, something you could feel but that you could not see. This idea was developed by John the Apostle:

"The wind bloweth where it listeth, and thou hearest the
sound thereof, but canst not tell whence it cometh and
wither it goeth; so is everyone that is born of the Spirit."
-John 3:8

God is not typically seen directly. Like the wind, we can see and feel the effects of God in our lives as we observe the effects of charitable service bestowed by one to another.

"Therefore we are always confident, knowing that, whilst
we are at home in the body, we are absent from the Lord.
(For we walk by faith, not by sight:) We are confident, I
say, and willing rather to be absent from the body, and
to be present with the Lord. Wherefore we labour, that,
whether present or absent, we may be accepted of him."
-2 Corinthians 5:6-9

Jesus addressed those concerns in one of the great ethical statements in history: "The Sermon On The Mount." We labor under the impression that our own personal issues are ours to bear all by ourselves. We presume that if we don't look out for ourselves, who will? But that ignores a benevolent God.

"…for your Father knoweth what things ye have need of,
before ye ask him."
-Matthew 6:8

Jesus then reinforces the idea that losing ourselves in the service of others includes a distancing of ourselves from concerns for our own sense of worldly well-being:

"Lay not up for yourselves treasures upon earth, where moth and rust doth corrupt, and where thieves break through and steal: But lay up for yourselves treasures in heaven, where neither moth nor rust doth corrupt, and where thieves do not break through nor steal: For where your treasure is, there will your heart be also."
-Matthew 6: 19-21

Jesus is speaking of the long-term perspective relative to what the desires of our hearts and minds should be. A happiness that comes from self-interest and attention pointed inward is neither rich nor durable. Joy, on the other hand, is eternal and comes from God. It lasts, and comes from tying yourself spiritually to others by serving them:

"Therefore, I say unto you, take no thought for your life, what ye shall eat, or what ye shall drink; nor yet for your body, what ye shall put on. Is not the life more than meat, and the body more than raiment? Behold the fowls of the air: for they sow not, neither do they reap, nor gather into barns; yet your heavenly father feedeth them. Are ye not much better than they? Which of you by taking thought can add one cubit unto his stature? And why take ye thought for raiment? Consider the lilies of the field, how they grow; they toil not, neither do they spin: And yet I say unto you, That even Solomon in all his glory was not arrayed like one of these. Wherefore, if God so clothe the grass of the field, which today is, and tomorrow is cast into the oven, shall he not much more clothe you, O ye of little faith? Therefore take no thought, saying, What shall we eat? or, what shall we drink? or, Wherewithal shall we be clothed? (For after all these things do the Gentiles seek:) for your heavenly Father knoweth that ye have need of all

these things. But seek ye first the kingdom of God, and his righteousness; and all these things shall be added unto you. Take therefore no thought for the morrow: for the morrow shall take thought for the things of itself. Sufficient unto the day is the evil thereof."
-Matthew 6: 25-34

GOD'S GIFT: JOY IN THIS WORLD AND THE NEXT

Joy is a gift from God. We can create happiness in our lives by our attitudes and responses to stimulus, but joy comes from God. It is eternal. Joy is the product of truly caring about and serving others.

> *"Joy, it seems, is not only happiness, but the resultant feeling of the Holy Ghost manifest within us."*
> -Barbara Winder, General Relief Society President of the Church of Jesus Christ of Latter-day Saints. *Ensign magazine.* Nov. 1987.

Joy does not come to all, but rather to those who care for others by acts of service. Joy is not something to be obtained simply by being or even by pursuing it for your own self-aggrandizement. Instead, caring, compassion, and charity seem to be the straight and narrow path to obtaining the blessing of joy from God.

Sometimes translations make a big difference in our understanding. A Bible verse is instructive:

> *"Glory to God in the highest, and on earth peace, good will toward men."*
> -Luke 2:14

The New Testament in the King James translation of the Bible speaks of the angels singing at Jesus Christ's birth, implying that good will was to be poured out on all. However, a different translation appears in *Don Quixote de la Mancha*. It reads:

> *"Glory to God in the highest and peace on earth to men of good will."*
> -Miguel de Cervantes, *Don Quixote de la Mancha*

By a seemingly insignificant transposition of words, that verse can be read in two very different ways. The first is that the peace that Jesus spoke of as His peace comes to all men. But that does not seem to be true given the state of the world as it is. Peace would hardly be applicable to many who are drowning in the world of war and hate. The second translation reported by Cervantes makes much more sense. In order to enjoy peace on earth you must be a person of good will. In other words, joy comes from acts of good will, practicing caring, compassion, and charity, and not from any other source. Jesus spoke of a peace that he was leaving with his disciples, a peace different than the world gives. That peace is the joy achieved when personal and worldly problems are set aside as we ease the burdens of those around us through service.

Author Albert Paine drew a rather stark distinction between what we do for ourselves and what we do for others:

> *"What we do for ourselves dies with us. What we do for others and the world is and remains immortal."*

Albert Einstein put it this way:

> *"Only a life lived for others is a life worthwhile."*

Our activities and actions that create pleasure and happiness for us in this life are of our own making. We cannot cash them in beyond the immediate generation of pleasure or happiness. We can have fond memories (or pain as the case may be) with our friends and acquaintances but we cannot tie those selfish indulgences to any eternal connection. Joy, on the other hand, is something that we actually transfer to someone else as our attention is focused on that someone else. When we relive happy times with friends, those who participated enjoy the revelry. But those who are hearing the story for the first time often respond with "I guess you had to be there to get it." By contrast, stories of caring, compassion, and charity can make anyone respond with warm feelings of joy.

There is a multiplier effect when we attend to the needs of others. It not only brings satisfaction to ourselves but also to those to whom we have directed our good works. Arguably then, when we utilize *caring, compassion, and charity* to address the needs of others, we are committing eternal acts where forward progression in life emerges, making everyone better. When we turn our *caring, compassion, and charity* outward toward the needs of others, we elevate our own standing:

*"To touch the soul of another human being is to walk on
holy ground."*
-Stephen R. Covey

*"I slept and dreamt that life was joy. I awoke and saw that
life was service. I acted and behold, service was joy."*
-Rabindranath Tagore

*"Now the God of hope fill you with all joy and peace in
believing, that ye may abound in hope, through the power
of the Holy Ghost."*
-Romans 15:13

God has set up a plan for us to achieve so much more than the happiness that we try to create for ourselves. He wishes joy for us. But to obtain joy, we must be willing to delegate our own selfish and worldly pursuit of happiness behind charity, so that we can both see and then attend to, the needs of our neighbors. Our inward focus must be turned out to everyone else in our spheres of influence. We need to lose ourselves in the service of our fellow man. In response, God will unleash joy in our lives. He has set forth His "mission statement" as follows:

> *"For behold, this is my work and my glory—to bring to*
> *pass the immortality and eternal life of man."*
> -Pearl of Great Price, *Moses 1: 39*

We exist to obtain joy. God has provided a pathway to joy which is to follow His commandments, the two most important of which are to love Him and to love His children. His reward to us is an eternal life of joy. Good works on behalf of others double back and inure to our ultimate good in this world and the next.

> *"The thief cometh not, but for to steal, and to kill, and to*
> *destroy: I am come that they might have life, and that they*
> *might have it more abundantly."*
> -John 10:10

There is a state of happiness we can aspire to and obtain; that is not a bad thing. But it is a limited thing. Its goal is to satisfy the natural man that resides in all of us. It comes from trying to satisfy our own needs and desires. Our attention is pointed inward. But God, with knowledge of our potential, has more in store for us than that. He has promised us joy, which comes from Him, not from within ourselves.

We obtain joy by lightening others' burdens, which means that we care, show compassion, and act with charity towards others.

EXPECT NOTHING IN RETURN

An insightful friend shared a thought that seems to have a practical application here:

"Happy [I think this should read 'joyful'] people are those who can give without remembering and receive without forgetting."
-Janet Anderson, Retired Principal, South Pasadena High School

We have all met with acquaintances who have given gifts in the form of objects, or service, who then for years worry about whether or not they were properly thanked and appreciated for their gift. Such a worry is for nothing. What was the purpose of the gift? Was it to make us look or feel good, or was it to make someone else happy? If our intention was to benefit others, then the reaction shouldn't much matter. (Of course, if the receiver's attention is properly pointed outward, then his or her natural reaction will be to be gracious. But that is his or her own problem). The bottom line is that the satisfaction, the reward for the gift, is the benefit bestowed by us because we love someone. Remember that the reward comes from the lifting of someone else's burden, not satisfying our own need for recognition.

*"We make a living by what we get. We make a life by
what we give."*
-Winston Churchill

*"What do we live for, if it is not to make life less difficult
for each other?"*
-George Eliot

*"The meaning of life is to find your gift. The purpose of life
is to give it away."*
-Pablo Picasso

Sometimes we need to not only put our own needs in a second-place position, but occasionally that means that our own self-interests need to be postponed indefinitely in order to address the needs of others. Pleasure's immediate gratification can often interfere with the long-term value of joy. Gordon B. Hinckley, former President of The Church of Jesus Christ of Latter Day Saints, made an interesting observation when he said:

*"The cause of most of man's unhappiness is sacrificing what
he wants most for what he wants now."*

What we want now is to be happy. What God has in store for us is joy. The challenge is to be patient enough and selfless enough to allow joy to come to us. "Happiness" we can pursue for ourselves and in our own time. "Joy" comes to us in God's time rather than according to our timetable.

It is not that we can never seek happiness. Neither is it necessary to abandon happiness for joy. Rather, it is the order of things that can make the difference. Priorities matter. Serving brings joy.

"Don't be afraid to give up the good and go for the great."
-Steve Prefontaine

*"You will come to know that what appears today to be a
sacrifice will prove instead to be the greatest investment
that you will ever make."*
-Gordon B. Hinckley

*"It is in our interest to take care of others. Self-centeredness
is opposed to basic human nature. In our own interest
as human beings we need to pay attention to our inner
values. Sometimes people think compassion is only of help
to others, while we get no benefit. This is a mistake. When
you concern yourself with others, you naturally develop a
sense of self-confidence. To help others takes courage and
inner strength."*
-Dalai Lama

"…can't forget we only get what we give."
-New Radicals, "You Get What You Give"

Lifting others' burdens is done for the benefit of our neighbors,
not for ourselves. But in the end, the outward focus results in benefits
to the giver. The giver's own troubles are diminished. Not that they
actually vanish, but they are brought into perspective.

The size of the burden to be lifted or the number of people involved
are not nearly as important as actually lifting. The great thing about
pursuing joy is that it doesn't take extreme measures, nor does it need to
impact lots of people all at once. Family members, friends, even perfect
strangers at the supermarket all can provide opportunities for service.

*"Never worry about numbers. Help one person at a time,
and always start with the person nearest you."*
-Mother Teresa

God will take care of our emotional needs once we have taken care
of our neighbors. In fact, Jesus warns about trying to gain from our
outward manifestations of love:

*"Take heed that ye do not your alms before men, to be seen of
them: otherwise ye have no reward of your Father which is in
heaven. Therefore when thou doest thine alms, do not sound
a trumpet before thee, as the hypocrits do in the synagogues
and in the streets, that they may have glory of men. Verily I
say unto you, they have their reward. But when thou doest
alms, let not thy left hand know what thy right hand doeth.
That thine alms may be in secret: and thy Father which seeth
in secret himself shall reward thee openly."*
-Matthew 6: 1-4

*"And if your eye be single to my glory, your whole bodies
shall be filled with light, and there shall be no darkness in
you; and that body which is filled with light comprehen-
deth all things."*
-Doctrine and Covenants 88:67

With the light that is promised and that comes with service,
joy follows:

*"But the fruit of the Spirit is love, joy, peace, long suf-
fering, gentleness, goodness, faith, meekness, temperance:
against such there is no law."*
-Galatians 5:22-23

Warmth and light are oftentimes used to describe feelings of joy. These terms are rarely used in conjunction with happy. Warmth and light are felt within. In religious terms, they emanate from the light of Christ:

"That which is of God is light; and he that receiveth light, and continueth in God, receiveth more light; and that light growth brighter and brighter until the perfect day"
-Doctrine and Covenants 50:24

God has promised light and joy when our *caring, compassion, and charity* are directed toward others. Accordingly, each time that our thoughts of the needs of others comes first, our own burdens are lifted:

"Come unto me, all ye that labour and are heavy laden, and I will give you rest. Take my yoke upon you, and learn of me; for I am meek and lowly in heart: and ye shall find rest unto your souls. For my yoke is easy, and my burden is light."
-Matthew 11: 28

In placing the needs of others first, above our own concerns and above our own life's issues and our own heartaches, we move toward the opportunity of living perfect days. John Wooden the legendary UCLA basketball coach, spoke of a perfect day this way:

"You can't live a perfect day without doing something for someone who will never be able to repay you."

JOY IN THE EVERY DAY

Service does not necessarily require life-altering sacrifice. It can come during the most mundane activities of everyday life. I have been required by my job to travel the Los Angeles freeway system daily. Some days the freeways are so congested that I give up and escape to surface streets which take longer but allow me to keep moving. This causes me to pass through neighborhoods that I would otherwise never see.

On one occasion, I was driving southbound on Atlantic Blvd. It was closing in on 5:30 p.m. and I was in need of a snack, as it would be another hour or more before I made it home. On the left-hand side of the road, I was approaching a McDonalds. I turned left into the strip mall lot and as I did, I saw a Walgreen's Pharmacy. The McDonalds looked crowded, so I decided on Walgreen's for a Diet Mountain Dew, Cheetos, and a Milky Way. Entering Walgreen's, sometime in March or April of that year, I saw a young boy, only four or five years old, with his young mother. The boy had a DVD of *Rudolph The Red-Nosed Reindeer* in his hands, begging his mother to buy it. She insisted to him that she didn't have enough money for the $4.99 DVD. By the look of things, I believed her.

I gathered my snacks, or should I say my evening meal, and got in the checkout line to pay. The mother and young boy got in line right behind me, and I could hear the boy continuing in his pleas for Rudolph, and his mother's apologetic and repeated responses that she could not afford it. Then, as if I had been pricked by a sharp object, I asked the young mother to hold my place in line and, without waiting for a response, left the line. I walked over to the DVD rack, picked up *Rudolph The Red-Nosed Reindeer*, returned to the line and waited to be checked out.

I paid for my snacks and the DVD. I then turned to the little boy and handed him the DVD without uttering a single word. His face looked up at me wondering what was happening at first. His quizzical look quickly transformed into a broad and grateful smile. I nodded at his mother and walked out of the Walgreen's.

Usually, I eat my "nutritious" snacks as I drive. But this time I just sat in the car, snacking and thinking. It felt so good, so warming to have cared about a child and his mother, to have perceived what might make their day a little brighter and realize that I could make that happen. It wasn't about me. It was about them, and it took so little effort. My snacks made me happy. But on this occasion, I looked outward and found joy. My troubles drifted from my mind. I was at peace…and all for only $4.99.

In the end, happiness isn't just a lesser degree of joy. The source of happiness is worldly and inwardly pointed. It is the result of our own pursuits, addressing our own needs first. It is temporary. Joy, on the other hand, isn't just deeper or greater happiness. It is our successful caring for others, feeling compassion to the extent of seeing needs outside of our own, and then charitably acting for the edification of another. It comes from the heart. Joy then comes as a form of payment from God in fulfillment of His unilateral contract with us. As we follow the admonition of Jesus Christ, to love God first and our neighbors (everyone you come into contact with) second, we leave our own concerns and perceived needs to God. That caring, compassion, and charity lead to a cascade of blessings from God, including a heavenly shield from the troubles of the world. Peace enters the heart, crowding out the demons of our lives.

Joy is the reward for our love of all God's children reflected in service. As we serve through caring, compassion, and charity, He will shoulder our burdens and replace them with light, joy, and His peace. The source of happiness is us. The source of joy is God. The difference couldn't be any more clear.

Still, our own self interests are always just a thought away. In our secular world, the promise of joy has somehow gotten lost in the brambles of everyday life. We often leave God out of the equation and replace Him with our own life's pursuit of self-interests. We are then resigned to the mantra that "I just want to be happy," which is a real loss.

God's promise of the gift of joy still stands. He waits for us to stop being so naive in our belief that we don't need Him. The alternative is that we are settling for the pittance of happiness that we can marshal for ourselves in this secular world. His hope is that we love our neighbors. If we do that, if we commit charity we can count on God to fulfill His promise to fill our lives with light and joy and the sweet peace that comes from knowing that we have helped another soul.

ACKNOWLEGEMENT

David Bartholomew approached me after a church talk I gave in our congregation in Laguna Beach, California and encouraged me to turn the talk into a book…this is that book. I am not sure that *Joy In The Brambles* happens without his kind words.

Overall, it took a village to keep pushing me in the right direction. Janet Tanner Perry read the first, rough draft. It took her a couple of weeks and all of the post-its that her local Staples could provide. When she handed the transcript back to me her question was: "This is a rough draft…isn't it?" Thankfully, it was. She suggested adding some stories to illustrate the points I was trying to make.

A stream of other readers verified stories and kept me from wandering into the weeds of unimportant tangents. My children and my wife, who know me well, were particularly helpful in keeping me out of the brambles and focused on joy. John Montgomery, Athelia Woolley, and Tony Ragucci all provided very helpful perspectives that helped form a more cohesive transcript.

The bottom line is that combining the many contributions from so many people who helped me with putting this work together along with those whose quotations and stories I utilized makes me seem to be more of a compiler/collator than an author.

After all of the help, I am sure there are more errors in grammar, punctuation, and structure. Those mistakes that remain are all mine.

I am grateful that there are many fewer mistakes than when I began. Thank you to so many for your contributions to this book specifically—and to my life generally.